GROWING UP LUTHERAN

What Does This Mean?

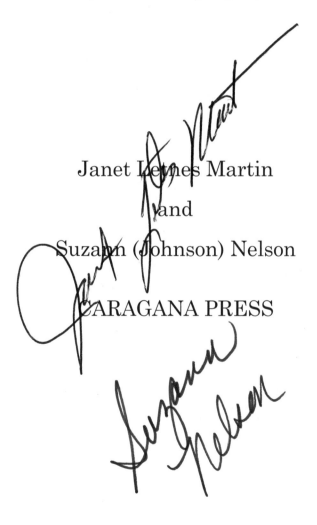

Janet Letnes Martin

and

Suzann (Johnson) Nelson

CARAGANA PRESS

CARAGANA PRESS
BOX 396
HASTINGS, MN 55033

Printed in the United States of America.

Published by Caragana Press
PO Box 396, Hastings, MN 55033

Library of Congress Catalog Card Number 97-069403

ISBN 1-886627-05-3

FIRST EDITION
Sixth Printing - 2003

Cover Design: Joe Gillaspie
Hastings, MN
Printer: Sentinel Printing,
St. Cloud, MN

Dedication

This book is dedicated to
all those who memorized the answers to:

What Does This Mean?

...and

How Is This Done?

To Our Readers

Dear Fellow Lutherans, Friends, & Fans,

For several years we have been planning to write a nostalgic book about growing up Lutheran. Since both of us are now 50 years old and not getting any younger, we decided we better get this written down or we would start to forget not only "what it meant" to be a Lutheran, but "how it was done." Part way through the project we realized we still had our faculties. We had too many memories, too much information, and too many photos (many of them from our readers and audiences) for one book. Whereas this is sort of a scrapbook of our memories, the next one will be primarily a photo album entitled *Picture This*. It will be filled with more memories of growing up Lutheran in the Midwest in the 50's. Feel free to submit interesting pictures to us.

We can, in all honesty, both say that we are experts on the topic of growing up Lutheran. We were both born in October '46 to Lutheran farm parents; Janet in North Dakota, and Suzann in Minnesota. We were both baptized into the Lutheran faith in November '46, and grew up attending Sunday School at different Our Savior's Lutherans. Both of us went to Lutheran Bible Camps, faithfully attended Luther League and Luther League Conventions, graduated from Augsburg (Lutheran) College, and repeated all of Luther's Small Catechism for our pastors in May '61. You could say we were saturated with the Lutheran heritage from the time we were born until we both married good Scandinavian Lutheran boys from rural areas. We're still wringing wet with it, and trying to pass it on to our children.

However, this book is not just an autobiography of *our* "Growing Up Lutheran" remembrances, nor is it a book written to poke fun of our Lutheran heritage. We both speak at hundreds of Lutheran churches of various synods throughout the nation each year, and countless Lutherans have related their endearing, often hilarious, stories. Many of those stories, and many related pictures, are included in this book and help capture the "Lutheran Experience."

By combining our memories and pictures with those of other Lutherans who grew up in the 40's through the 60's, our book is like an old-fashioned Lutheran church basement hotdish. We have put together a mixture of ingredients that we had on hand, generously salted it with gentle humor, and lightly peppered it with quite a few hot granules of Lutheran theology.

This is most certainly true.

Janet Letnes Martin and Suzann (Johnson) Nelson

Contents

Part One: What Does This Mean?

Part Two: How Is This Done?

Part One:
What Does This Mean?

And His Name Shall Be Called Gilman Einar Stedje

And His Name Shall Be Called Gilman Einar Stedje

A child didn't become a real Lutheran until he was baptized in a Lutheran setting. Some Lutheran babies who were born in a Catholic-run hospital were secretly baptized by the good nuns, but Lutherans knew that this didn't count.

Lutherans, who have always been frugal, have never believed in doing things to excess. This, coupled with the fact that so many Lutherans settled on the prairies, led to the BryllCream theory of Baptism. Unlike the Baptists who were totally submersed, Lutherans believed that "a lil dab'll do ya."

Good Lutheran parents baptized their babies:

- when the relatives could make it, and
- before the child got too big.

Normally Lutherans baptized their babies at about four to eight weeks old. If they waited any longer, parishioners' tongues would wag and conscientious Lutheran parents would feel the chill coming from the pews. In other words, it wasn't "suffer the little children," but suffer the parents who should have known better than to wait so long—especially if the baby fussed and acted up during the Baptism.

Children of the
Heavenly Father

458 Black
572 Red
474 Green

The confirmed Lutheran relatives, who stood up at the Baptismal font with the parents and who were invited over for dinner after the services, were usually called sponsors.*

Some people, especially those who had family members who had married outside of their faith, called sponsors "godparents," but for most Lutherans the word, godparent, sounded too much like something the "Fish on Friday" crew would say and conjured up thoughts of the mob and the Mafia. Thus, Lutherans were more comfortable with the term, sponsors. Sponsors were usually in their 20's or 30's. Any older and most Lutherans felt one would be taking chances at not having them around for Confirmation.

Most girls who were baptized Lutheran in the 40's or 50's were given a sensible, pronounceable first name like Jean, Janet, or Judy. Their second name was usually given to honor an older, deserving relative. These were names like Helen, Alice, or Mae. Girls received either a cross on a chain or a spoon as a gift from their sponsors. Usually they were baptized in a modest little white dress. Invariably, it was new because there wasn't anything left over from the Depression to pass down. Boys who were baptized Lutheran usually got a couple of bucks in a nice card from their sponsors and were named after their dad or one of the grandparents. They had names like Einar, Emil, or Edward. They were normally dressed in a little pale blue suit which was bought locally—probably at the Johnson Store.

The church furnished a Baptismal Certificate signed by the pastor. Since most Lutherans didn't deem it necessary to take any pictures at Baptism, the certificate is the only memento they have. To this day, most Lutherans keep their certificate with their LB or AAL insurance policies in a safe, dry place.

This is most certainly true.

**If it was the Baptism of the third or fourth child, the parents often skipped having the sponsors over for dinner. That was okay though, because these babies didn't have a baby book or baby picture either. Often there was no picture of these children until they began mandatory attendance at public school. Not having these special baby frills wasn't because the parents loved these children any less; it's just the way it was.*

Blessed Assurance

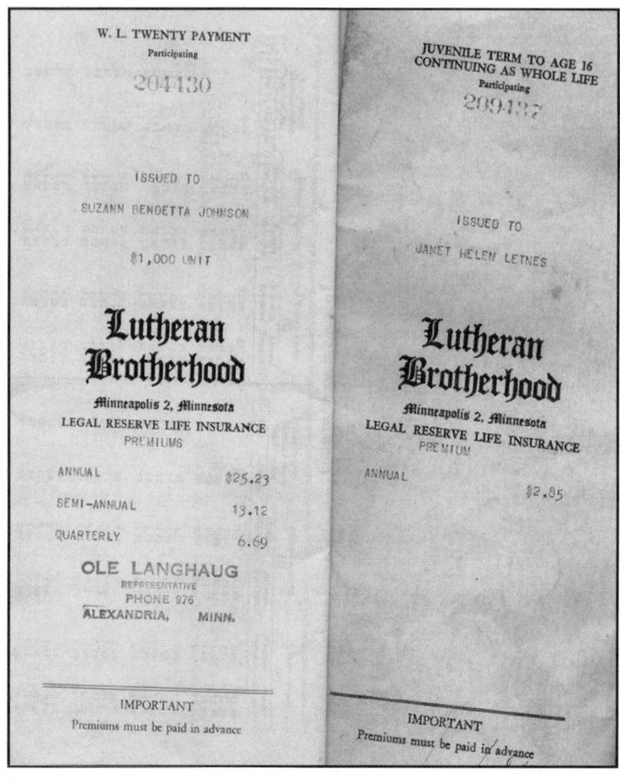

W. L. TWENTY PAYMENT
Participating
204130

ISSUED TO
SUZANN BENDETTA JOHNSON
$1,000 UNIT

Lutheran Brotherhood
Minneapolis 2, Minnesota
LEGAL RESERVE LIFE INSURANCE

PREMIUMS

ANNUAL	$25.23
SEMI-ANNUAL	13.12
QUARTERLY	6.69

OLE LANGHAUG
REPRESENTATIVE
PHONE 976
ALEXANDRIA, MINN.

IMPORTANT
Premiums must be paid in advance

JUVENILE TERM TO AGE 16
CONTINUING AS WHOLE LIFE
Participating
209437

ISSUED TO
JANET HELEN LETNES

Lutheran Brotherhood
Minneapolis 2, Minnesota
LEGAL RESERVE LIFE INSURANCE

PREMIUM

ANNUAL	$2.85

IMPORTANT
Premiums must be paid in advance

Blessed Insurance

Excerpts from the Bulletin

The Lutheran Brotherhood Agent reminds you to make sure your beneficiaries are current.

Little Lutherans in Limbo

Chapter One
OUR FAMILY
I belong to our family. When my father and mother were married, they promised God to live together in love all their life. When I came to them I was very small and helpless, but they said I helped them just because I was their baby. We promise to love and help one another all our life long. Our family's name
Mr & Mrs Theodo
(Name)
We live in
Evansville
(City)
Chapter Two
GOD'S GREAT FAMILY
I belong to God's great family — the Church. When Jesus was a baby, Mary and Joseph brought Him to God's house and gave Him to God. My parents gave me to God when I was baptized on
Nov. 24th - 1946. They promised
(Date-Year)
keep me His child. Our friends
Mrs Milo Stamness
Lerum & Donna Urness
(God-Parents and Sponsors)
lp. The name of our church is
Luth. Church
CRADLE ROLL CERTIFICATE
The Story of Me

Little Lutherans in Limbo

After a child was baptized Lutheran, but before they started Sunday School, the cry room crew got enrolled—for one dollar—in the local church's chapter of the Lutheran Women's Missionary Federation which had headquarters located at Minneapolis 15, Minn.

Even though cradle roll was meant to interest Lutheran children in missionary work, most Lutheran children were too young to know that there were heathens in Alaska who hadn't seen the light yet. As Mrs. Byron C. Nelson wrote in a 1939 tract published by the Literature Committee of the Women's Missionary Federation of the Norwegian Lutheran Church in America, these dollars helped finance an adult missionary who worked "among their fur-robed brothers of the North," and who would "hazard the icy North" to do outreach work for the little Lutheran missionaries back home who couldn't yet walk.

Once these little Lutherans got old enough to think, they never thought much about Cradle Roll because there were never any Catechization questions pertaining to it.

Mothers of Cradle Roll children received tracts and pamphlets on the missionary work that the Cradle Roll supported. Even though children were dropped from the rolls when they started Sunday School, Cradle Roll membership was

the second rite of passage for Lutherans.

Somewhere between joining Cradle Roll and leaving for the mission field in Alaska, many Lutheran kids—especially those in their Terrible Two's—spent some time in the cry room. Just as the Catholics had limbo, a place for unbaptized babies located somewhere between heaven and hell, the Lutherans who went to town churches had the Cry Room, a place for fussy babies located in the back of the church.

Lutherans have no direct recollection of being in the Cradle Roll or the Cry Room. They learn about Cry Rooms (now called Nurseries) when they have children of their own, and about Cradle Roll when they are middle-aged and go through the stuff that their parents saved and find their Cradle Roll Certificate in with old nut cups left over from Mother-Daughter Teas and yellowing mimeographed

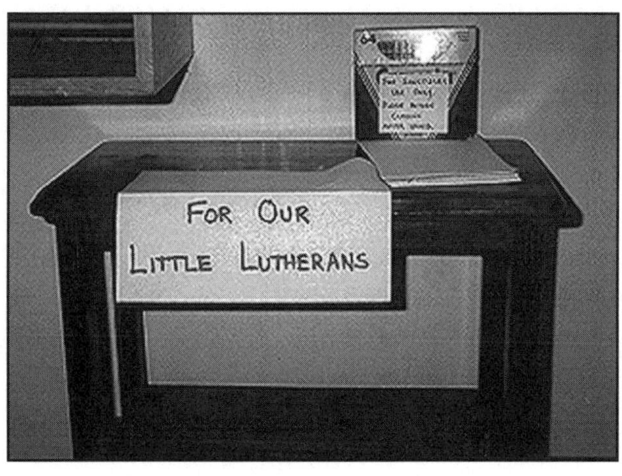

pictures of pilgrims that had been colored in third grade.

Along with the Certificate, these middle-aged Cradle Roll graduates know they belonged to Cradle Roll because they have birthday cards (from their first through third birthdays) from the local branch of the WMF glued in their scrapbooks to prove it.

This is most certainly true.

Little Missionaries to Alaska in Cradle Caps

Excerpts from the Bulletin

For Family Night next week, Roger Helleckson, home on a six-month furlough, will be here to show a filmstrip about the work he is doing on the Mission Field in North Borneo. The week after that, Selma Rorvik will talk about her trip to Norway.

Now I Lay Me

Now I lay me
Down to sleep,
I pray the Lord
My soul to keep.
If I should die*
Before I wake,
I pray the Lord
My soul to take.

**This is why little Lutherans don't sleep very much.*

Let all the Earth Keep Silence Befo-ore Him

Let all the Earth Keep Silence Befo-ore Him

One hour every Sunday morning from Labor Day to Memorial Day, Lutheran children between the ages of three and 18 gathered in church basements across the nation to sing and to pray, to memorize and to play. It was Sunday School time!

Lutheran parents, from the regular steadfast "you-can-always-count-on-them-being-there pillar types" down to the Christmas-Easter attendees who stayed away 50 weeks of the year because "there are just too many hypocrites sitting in the pew," made sure their children faithfully attended Sunday School. Many of the pillars were busy teaching while the Christmas-Easter folks were sitting in cars outside the church reading the Sunday paper.

For children of the pillar types, Sunday School began on Saturday night with a bath followed by the parents' proverbial question, "Do you have your lessons learned?" and the statement, "Let me hear your memory work."

After the milking was done Sunday morning, breakfast was eaten and nickels were tied in the corner of hankies for the Sunday School offering. The Lutheran families in the regular steadfast faction dressed all up: mom in her good girdle, hat, gloves and Sunday dress; dad in his only suit, a white shirt, tie and hat; and children in their church clothes—boys in a two-piece suit that mom lowered the cuffs on monthly, and girls in a Sunday dress and Sunday shoes with clean, white anklets in the summer and long, white stockings hung onto a garter belt in the winter. They went off to church to get their weekly religion and have some coffee.

The children were brought to the church basement by their parents. After they removed their coats and overshoes, they quietly sat down in their rows on little red or brown chairs placed in and amongst the church basement poles to wait for the superintendent to say, "Good morning, children. This is the day that the Lord has given. We will open by singing *The Lord Is In His Holy Temple, Let All the Earth Keep Silence, Keep Silence Befo-ore Him."* It was a good song because it let the children of the Christmas—Easter types know that in this setting there would be no shuffling feet, poking, or any other type of monkey business. Following the opening song, little Lutherans bowed their heads, folded their hands, and closed their eyes for an Opening Prayer. Other than an occasional offering nickel rolling on the floor, all was silent.

Opening Exercise continued with more songs like *Jesus Loves Me* and *This Little Light of Mine;* a little lesson about moral issues like sharing, helping and not hitting; and the offering which was sent to foreign mission fields. Before the closing prayer, Lutheran children who were having birthdays the following week got to come to the front of the room to put their pennies (one for each year of life) into the birthday bank. While the superintendent or her "pet" held the bank, the children who were sitting in their chairs sang *Happy Birthday.* The Lutheran birthday child was in glory because it was a wonderful, non-bragging Lutheran way to let everyone else know that it was his day to shine!

After the closing prayer, the children and their teachers were excused row by row (starting at the front) and sent to their individual learning centers—some in the kitchen, some enclosed behind Sunday School dividers or curtains, and the older ones to the furnace room. After attendance was taken and recorded, Lutheran children learned about

Daniel in the den of lions, and saw stories enacted on flannelgraph boards. They recited memory work and got gold, blue, or red stars for learning it by heart. Towards the end of the hour when the teacher saw that no one was paying attention anymore, she put away her books and let the children color Joseph's coat of many colors or play with blocks and clay while they waited for their parents to pick them up.

Lutheran children with perfect attendance spent 540 hours of their lives in Sunday School. Each year the Sunday School recognized those who had perfect attendance or had only missed one or two Sundays due to measles, mumps, chicken pox or the Asiatic flu. These conscientious Lutheran children received either a certificate, little book, pin, wreath, or a bar to attach to their Sunday School pin for being so diligent.

Lutherans didn't fully complete this third rite of passage until they graduated from high school, were honored at the Senior Sunday School Banquet and were no longer required to attend Sunday School—only to teach it.

This is most certainly true.

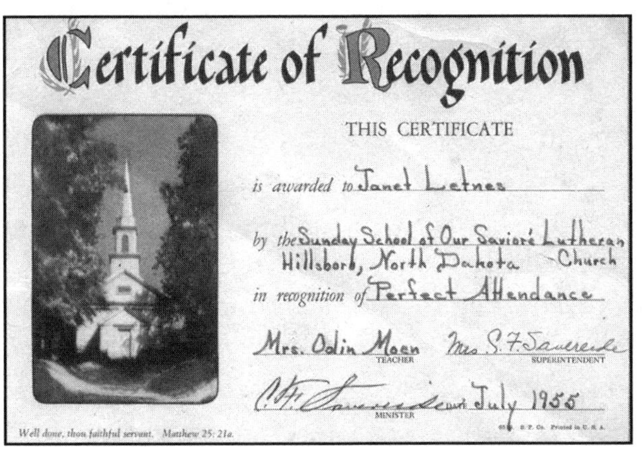

Certificate of Recognition

THIS CERTIFICATE

is awarded to Janet Letnes

by the Sunday School of Our Savior's Lutheran Church
Hillsboro, North Dakota

in recognition of Perfect Attendance

Mrs. Odin Moen — TEACHER

[illegible] — SUPERINTENDENT

July 1955 — MINISTER

Well done, thou faithful servant. Matthew 25:21a.

The Best Bathrobe Pageant Ever

Planning for the Sunday School Christmas Program started in earnest around the middle of October when the Sunday School superintendent started to line things up in a notebook as well as in her head.

September was always taken up with the average basic Sunday School organizational problems such as where in the world to put all the kids, how to recruit more teachers, who will reorder more Sunday School material, etc.—and harvest.

The real work for the teacher began in November when the Sunday School superintendent called a meeting to tell them what the program was about, who was Mary, (either her daughter or the pastor's daughter), and who was Joseph (either the pastor's son or someone else who was decent and would work out). She enlisted the teachers to help her pick out the wisemen, shepherds, and angels. She needed kids in these parts who not only would behave and follow directions, but ones who were tall enough so they wouldn't trip on the costumes. Of course, the chosen had to have parents who were dependable enough to get them to practices, and to get them there on time. The costumes, mostly old bathrobes, were dug out of the storeroom at this time and quickly checked over for mending or approval.

The real work for the children started in November, too. After Reformation Sunday, Opening Exercise was taken up with learning one new Christmas song and the second and third verses to familiar ones. They were sung over and over and over again. Right after Thanksgiving the teachers sent home "the pieces" that the children had to memorize. Also after Thanksgiving, Saturday morning practices started and continued in full force until the week of the program.

These practices left the superintendent dizzy, the teachers in a tizzy, and the kids just wanting to get out of there. The superintendent, like Zacchaeus, was up a tree. She would yell from the back of the church that she couldn't hear the kids as they stumbled through their pieces. The shepherds and wisemen, bored as could be, started to fool around which got the superintendent yelling even louder. The sweet little angels even got on her nerves. Parents would bring their kids late to practice, pick them up early, and some didn't even bother to get them there at all.

However, at the last practice before the program things got worse. This was usually a full dress rehearsal and anything that could go wrong did. The mothers of the angels had cut the cardboard refrigerator box wings too large and the angels couldn't get down the side aisles. Joseph was allergic to the hay and continued to sneeze and wheeze until they had to grab a replacement. Mary said she didn't feel good because her white sheet and blue veil were so hot and itchy she felt like throwing up. The superintendent told her to sit down in the pew for a while but reassured her she would be just fine at the program. One of the shepherds tripped on his bathrobe and ripped it from the pocket down. One of the wisemen had a head that was too big for the crown so a replacement had to be made, wasting tin foil. Nobody knew when to stand, where to sit, or when to sing. One of the mothers who was helping out and had had some musical training noticed that the piano hadn't been tuned. A leg on the manger–which had seen its better days–was wobbly, and the blanket for the doll hadn't been washed since it was put away the year before. By the time the rehearsal was finished, it was the kids, not the cattle, who were lowing, and the superintendent vowed to herself that this was her last year.

But come time for the program, the hustle, bustle, and headaches were well worth it. The children came dressed to the hilt in their new Christmas outfits. Except for one three-year-old who announced to the whole church that he had to go potty, and another one who yelled "Hi, Mommy" at the top of his lungs, everything went off without a hitch. The three-year-olds knew most of the words and hand movements to *Away in a Manger*, and the older kids mostly had their long pieces down pat.

After the program, the pastor always gave a little meaningful talk that was directed to the children.

> "Boys and girls. That was one of the best programs ever. I'm confident you'll always remember the real meaning of Christmas. Now when you go home and look at your Christmas lights, remember that the white lights remind you of Christ's holiness and purity and that everyone in Heaven is dressed in white. The blue lights should remind you of the sky and blue water created by God who leads us beside the still waters. The green lights should remind you of the grace and love of God as well as the green grass written about in Psalm 23. The yellow bulbs remind us of the glory of Christ, and the red ones remind us of the blood of Christ and our redemption."

(At this time the pastor tells the children that red is his favorite color. Of course, this was before the hymnal controversy of 1959-1961.) "Purple lights," he continued, "remind us of Christ's suffering and that Pilate's soldiers put a purple robe on Him to ridicule Him, but purple also reminds us of royalty."

After the little sermonette, the pastor thanked the superintendent for all her work. The whole congregation—if it was ELC—then sang *Jeg er så glad*. The Augustana Synod churches, the ALC ones, sang *När juldagsmorgon glimmar*. Then the ushers turned the lights off and everyone sang *Silent Night*. (If it was a German-based congregation like the Missouri or Wisconsin Synod ones, this was sung in German as *Stille Nacht*.)

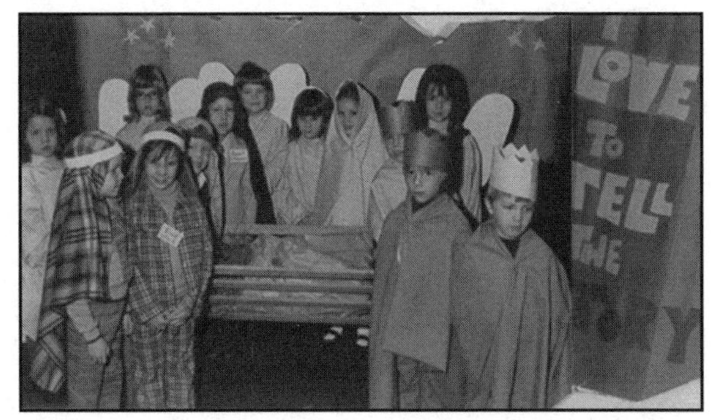

As the lights came on again, the children were excused to the basement* where each child received a gift from either the Sunday School or the congregation—a brown paper bag almost filled with unsalted peanuts in the shell, a red shiny apple, ribbon candy that stuck to the peanuts, and haystack-shaped chocolate drops that stuck to everything and smeared up new Christmas outfits. The teachers usually received gifts of boxed hankies, stationery, or nylons; Avon Wild Rose sachet, Topaz cream or Here's My Heart spray cologne; Watkins vanilla or carbo-salve; bath crystals, or crocheted book markers from their students.

The annual Sunday School Program, the highlight of the year for little Lutherans and their proud parents, was over. The fathers went out to warm up the cars while the kids found their boots, mittens, hats and snowpants and forgot their pieces. Beaming mothers ignored the chocolate-smeared new Christmas outfits and helped the now-relieved Sunday School superintendent pack up the costumes. All the families finally left the church excited about the coming of the Christ Child, but scared to death of sliding in the ditch with their nice clothes on.

This is most certainly true.

**In churches that were having a tough time meeting year-end expenses, the heat was kept turned down in the basement so the children remained seated in their pews for the distribution of the bags. Every year the conscientious teachers had packed just enough bags so that visiting children, the recently widowed, and each bachelor in attendance also received a bag of treats.*

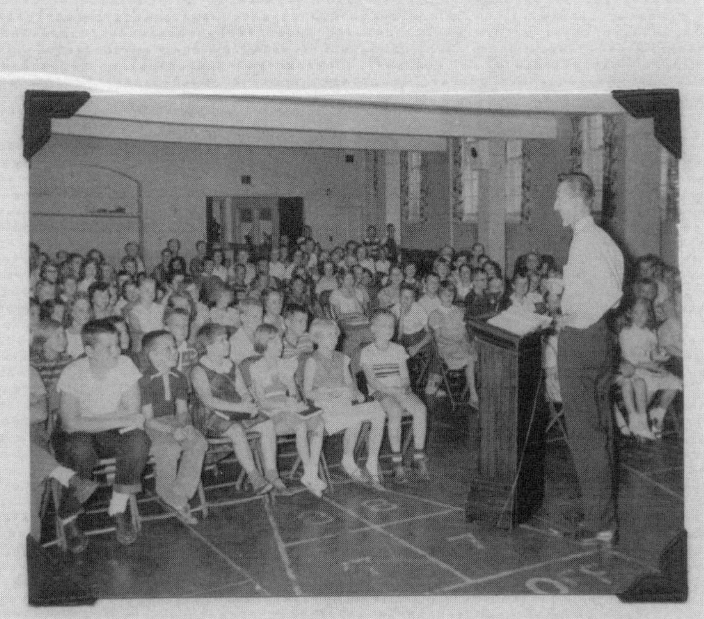

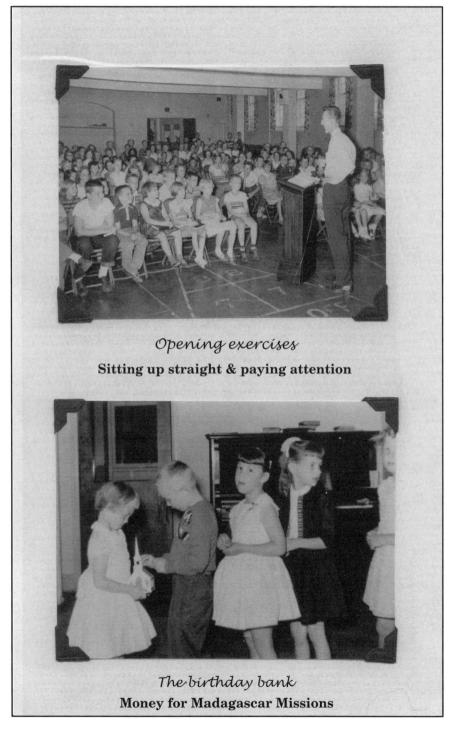

Opening exercises

Sitting up straight & paying attention

The birthday bank

Money for Madagascar Missions

Getting down to business

"Teacher, teacher. I know, I know."

Variety is the spice of life

A filmstrip instead of memorization

Reading the "begats"

Lutherans Cutting Loose on Sunday Morning

Right up there in importance with the Sunday School Christmas Program was the annual year-end Sunday School Picnic. After 36 weeks of sitting still, paying attention, memorizing everything from the Books of the Bible to numerous passages of scripture, and listening to fire and brimstone sermons, Lutheran children were introduced to Lite Lutheranism, i.e., a guilt-free, fun-packed, dressed-down Sunday morning service in the park or on the church grounds with games (led by the Leaguers), ice cream, watermelon, and a short, light sermon. It was at one of these annual Sunday School picnics that Herb Schultz, a little German Lutheran, summed up the feelings of many Lutheran children when he asked his mom, "Is this what it feels like to be a Congregationalist?" Herb's mom glared at him and told him to hold his tongue or he wouldn't get any ice cream. Even though he didn't understand why this would upset her, he didn't ask her any more deep theological questions.

It was a real disappointment to the children if it rained because then the picnic was held in the church basement and there were no gunny sack races, no tug of war games, and it was just plain no fun. It was short and polite and there wasn't any place to spit watermelon seeds. As the young Schultz boy said to his friend, Gerhard, in the year that "the rains came down and the floods went up", i.e., 1951, "A guy can't tell if this is a picnic or a funeral."

However, if the sun was out and the grounds were dry, the Lutherans let loose. Dads wore shirts without a tie or suitcoat. Girls wore pedal pushers and sleeveless crop tops. Boys wore comfortable school pants without fearing that they would get chewed out for getting grass stains on the knees, and even the pastor shed his jacket—but not his collar. Even though the women still wore dresses and nylons, the dresses were of the everyday variety (cotton instead of Dacron or linen) and the heels had been exchanged for wedgies.

The women prepared the potluck meal of hot dish, escalloped potatoes and ham, potato salad, pork and beans, Jell-O, buttered buns, pickles, watermelon, and Watkins orange nectar or lemonade. Usually the men scooped out the ice cream which was packed in five-gallon containers and stored in olive green, padded cases which prevented it from melting too fast. (These containers often showed up several months later at a bazaar camouflaged as decorative wastebaskets.) Some Lutheran churches took the lazy way out and served their ice cream in Dixie cups that were eaten with throwaway wooden tongue depressors. Everyone sat on blankets on the ground to eat, and then the men used these same blankets to snooze on. The women cleaned up, the men who weren't napping played horseshoe, and even the pastor had a good time.

This is most certainly true.

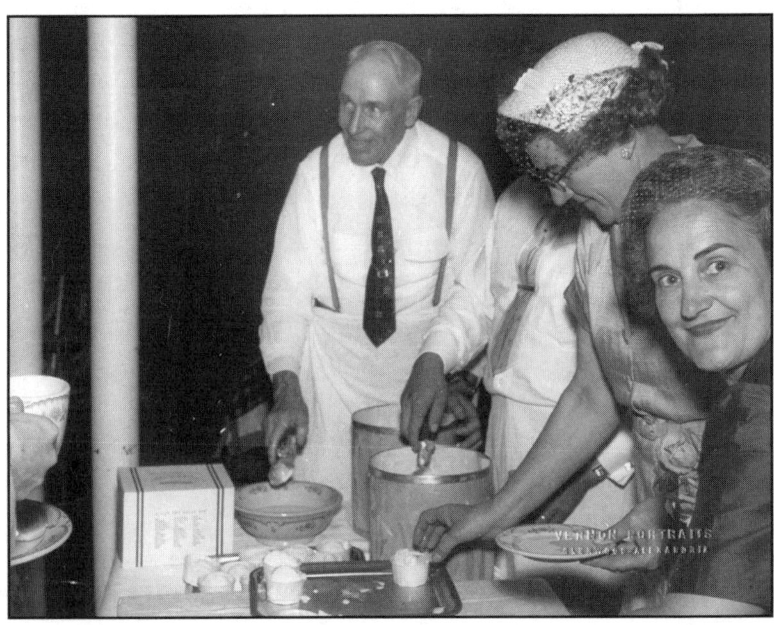

Parochial School: Reading, Writing, Dr. Martin Luther and Basketball

Not all Lutheran children went to public school. Hundreds of Lutheran children with last names like Schultz, Schmidt, and Lorenz were learning What Does This Mean and How Is This Done in Lutheran parochial schools. These Lutheran Missouri Synod Schools, sometimes referred to as "Ja, you know he went to one of those German Schools with the good basketball teams," are located mostly in the Midwest. (Kids at these schools learn about Dr. Martin Luther. The Scandinavian Lutherans, generally known for its low-church leanings, call him simply Martin Luther.)

As of today, German kids continue to enroll in parochial schools and their mothers are still serving kraut and sausage suppers to pay for more basketball hoops. Those German kids sure know how to dribble!

This is most certainly true.

Things Little Lutherans Ponder Upon in Their Hearts and Minds

If babies come from God, why was it so bad that the Swenson girl had one?

What does it feel like to dance?

Are there Lutherans in the South and Baptists in the North?

What does a bunch of heathens really act like, anyway?

How can three people be one person?

If we're supposed to pray without ceasing, how do we pray when we are sleeping, and how do you concentrate when you're driving?

If pride is bad, why is grandma so proud of me?

Why should I even want to covet my neighbor's ox?* And, do they even have any?

Does God still see everything you are doing when you are married? Do your dead relatives too, or don't they watch?

If we're not supposed to use bad words, why do we pray "Lead a snot into temptation?"

If I get paid a nickel for trapping gophers, how do I give 1/10 of it to church?

If Holy Rollers speak in tongues, is it German, Norwegian or Swedish?

If drinking alcohol is a sin, why do you guys have wine at communion?

If envy and jealousy are wrong, why is our God a jealous God?

If the iniquities of our fathers are visited onto the third and fourth generations, will it be okay for my great, great grandchildren to dance and play cards? What does this mean anyway?

**The invention of tractors took away some potential sins.*

Words that Scare the B'Jeebers Out of Little Lutherans

Belie	Betray	Backbite
Malice	Temptations	Blasphemy
False	Grievous	Perils
Vile	Faint	Weary
Shame	Unbelief	Vex
Tribulation	Defeat	Pestilence
Plague	Famine	Tempest
Stumbling	Vengeance	Greed
Temporal Things	Wrath	Fear
Transgress	Beseech	Venom
Evil Desires	Evil Devices	Flesh
Laziness	Gluttony	Deceit
Lust	Hatred	Envy
Enmity	Perfidy	Wicked Foe
Cursing	Reviling	Reproach
Slander	Arrogance	Serpents
Vindication	Wormwood and the Gall	

Stricken, Smitten and Afflicted

Lutherans also grew up with a general disdain for—if not full terror of—snakes and dust. (This most likely comes from the art work accompanying the Garden of Eden story in the King James Version, and the graveside Burial of the Dead Service.) Most Lutherans still have these feelings.

> *Excerpts from the Bulletin*
>
> There will be an emergency meeting this afternoon at 2:30 to discuss the condition of the furnace in the parsonage.

HYMNS FOR
SUNDAY SCHOOL

Into my Heart
The Lord is in His Holy Temple
Praise Him, Praise Him
The B-I-B-L-E
Jesus Loves the Little Children

We Give Thee but Thine Own
(for offering)

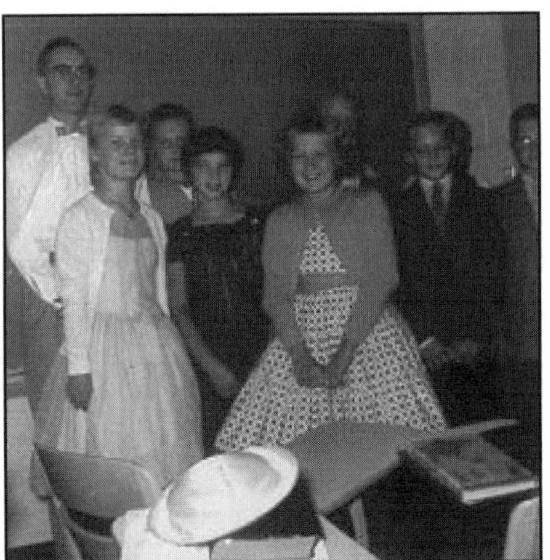

Willing Workers: From the kitchen to the classroom

Vacation Bible School and
Released Time

A Week of Sundays

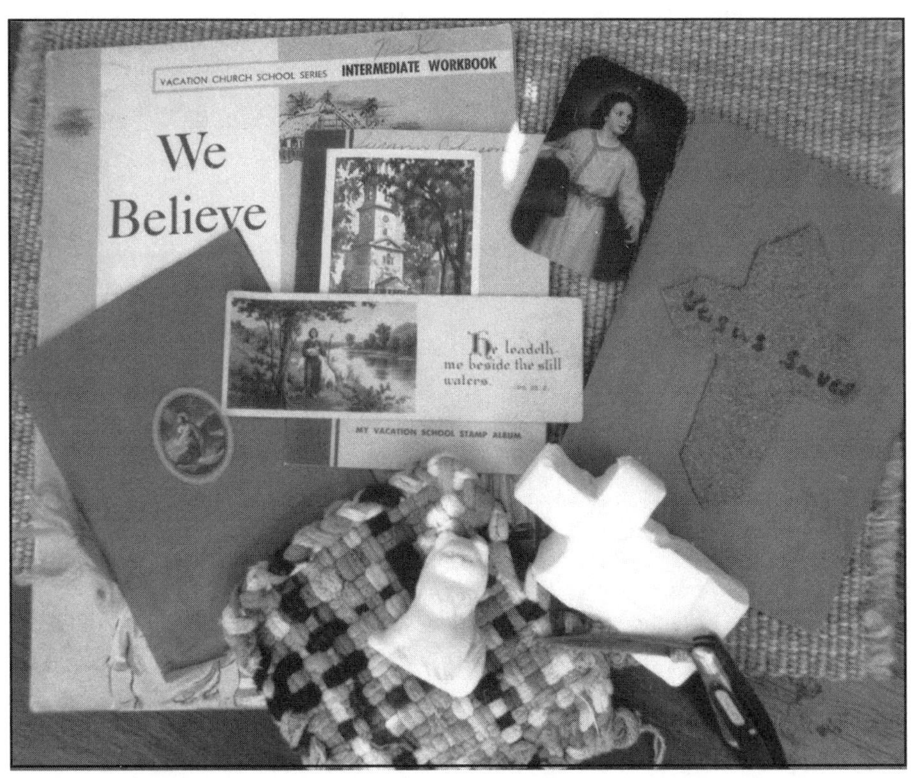

A Week of Sundays

Vacation Bible School: A week of Sundays — Kinda

More fun than Sunday School, but not as fun as the Sunday School picnic, Vacation Bible School was the fourth rite of passage for Lutheran children. VBS wasn't actually a vacation from learning and memorizing, but rather it was a vacation from public school, farm work for the country boys, and cleaning for the girls.

When the lilacs were in full bloom, but before the dandelions had gone to seed and the ditches needed mowing, Lutheran children gathered in the church basement for one week of full days or two weeks of half days (depending on the congregation) to study, memorize, and enjoy more sophisticated crafts than they did in Sunday School—crafts such as carving Holy Bibles out of Ivory soap bars, carving crosses out of cork, weaving key chains out of plastic lanyards, and making interesting things out of popsicle sticks. VBS was more casual than Sunday School, too. Girls could wear skirts or pedal pushers and never wore a dress to VBS unless it was a sundress.

Vacation Bible School was taught by mothers, and the nectar and lunch were served by the older Lutheran women who were getting up in age but still able to get around and help out. Even though the atmosphere was more relaxed than Sunday School, there were still mountains of memory work and pages of workbooks to fill out, all centered around a theme of the week selected by Augsburg Publishing House.* VBS music was livelier than it was in Sunday School, and Lutheran kids even learned how to sing *I will make you Fishers of Men* in Swahili.

The children especially enjoyed having a real recess at church. Town VBS children played Drop the Hanky and Ring Around the Rosey while rural VBS'ers fought for the cylinder-shaped tombstones to ride horsey on.

This is most certainly true.

** In 1957, Lutheran kids across the nation who went to churches that subscribed to Augsburg Publishing House materials memorized:*

Monday	*Psalm 105:1*
Tuesday	*Psalm 100:2*
Wednesday	*Psalm 111:1*
Thursday	*Psalm 75:1*
Friday	*Psalm 55:17*
Saturday	*Psalm 119:16*

Augsburg had selected Praise Him, Serve Him, Thank Him as the theme of the week, and Scandinavian mothers—showing off their knack for organizing, categorizing, and coordinating things—had selected "Praise Him, Praise Him...(Serve Him, Serve Him; Thank Him, Thank Him), All Ye Little Children" as the song of the week.

TOP 5 VBS SONGS

The B-I-B-L-E
We are Climbing Jacob's Ladder
The Wiseman Built his House
For God So Loved the World
I Will Make You Fishers of Men
Climb, Climb Up Sunshine Mountain

Released for the Lord

Many Lutheran kids spent an hour during the week at Released Time. This wasn't as much fun as either Sunday School or Vacation Bible School, but it was a good way to get out of school for a while. It was sort of a midweek booster shot.

While Protestant kids walked or were bused to the closest non-Catholic church, the Catholics were driven by their mothers to St. Agnes Parish Hall. Methodists, Covenant kids, and Baptists joined the Lutherans for this hour, and the unfortunate children from unchurched families could choose to join the Lutheran group, the Catholic kids, or could stay in the public school classroom with their teacher. The unchurched generally went with the group whose church was the farthest away from the schoolhouse. Permission slips were filled out in the Fall and the commitment ran for all nine months, unless a kid's school marks started to suffer.

Generally Released Time classes were intense; loads of memory work, but for the Lutheran kids it was good preparation for Confirmation classes.

The Catholics were taught by the nuns. Often the Lutheran teachers were sort of "professional" lay people. They had received lots of special training and, in the hierarchy, they were situated above the Sunday School teachers but below a deaconess. They were on a level with the Sunday School superintendent and the organist.

A typical class would open with prayer. Lutheran kids preferred silent prayer, but sometimes the teachers called for spontaneous or voluntary prayer,* but this got the Lutheran classes off to a slow start so usually the teacher led the prayer. A hymn—a fun one, not a black hymnal one—would follow. Sometimes the kids got carried away and the bulk of the hour was spent singing kids' choices, sort of the Top Twenty of Lutheran youth. Of course, the teacher liked this because it took the pressure off her but after about 11 songs, guilt set in and the teacher got down to business.

Business would include a Bible story, practicing Bible verses off flashcards, or a flannelgraph lesson about the heathens in Tanganyika for the younger classes, Old Testament history for the fifth and sixth graders, a what-does-this-mean-for-your-life-today discussion on an assigned New Testament chapter for the junior high kids, and a discussion group for the dwindling, but deadly serious, senior high group. These, the deadly ones, had already been confirmed but were still eager or obligated to learn more. At Released Time, they were often taught by an area minister.

Following the lesson, kids might have a Bible Race. This was like a spelling bee, but the point was to be the first to find a certain passage in the Bible. Spelling only counted in finding the right book of the Bible before others did. Of course, the kids with indexed margins always won, and those who had to use the hard-covered black Bibles donated by the Gideons always lost.

Occasionally a visiting missionary would be present and the non-Catholic kids learned about African drums, silk kimonos or water buffalo. Viewing pictures of the heathens that the missionaries brought along often gave Lutheran kids a chance to see more skin than they were used to seeing. This, too, was a learning experience.

The boys in the last class of the day helped the teacher rearrange the room for the next scheduled event while the girls put away the Concordias, pencils and bulletin boards.

A special "party" took place during the Released Time class closest to Christmas. Musical chairs were played or a film strip was shown. The teacher would give each of her students a candy cane and a religious bookmarker. Each year in November, right after the kids had learned about Martin Luther and the Reformation, the teacher announced that the children shouldn't give her any Christmas gifts but instead, if they felt so moved, could bring some money for a special offering to go to a designated mission field. But each year, the kids would give the teacher an assortment of new plastic holiday corsages, hankies, boxes of stationary, candy or nylons, crocheted crosses and kid-woven potholders, gloves, neck scarves, pins (generally the safest jewelry to give a Lutheran woman), or homemade jelly—all Lutheran versions of gold, frankincense and myrrh. And, each year they also brought a little extra for the missions. This, of course, guaranteed that at one of the classes in February or March—before Released Time classes took on the themes of Lent—the class would receive a thank-you from the missionaries, along with some photographs of the natives. This would give the Lutheran kids a chance to learn about far off places across the ocean and they would go home that night thankful that they only had to slop the hogs, not put ointment on the open sores of the lepers.

This is most certainly true.

**Luther Leaguers at national conventions called these popcorn prayers. They'd just pop out.*

THE NEW COMBINED BIBLE DICTIONARY AND CONCORDANCE
BAKER
Behlmer FROM TEENS TO MARRIAGE Concordia
CHRISTIAN MARRIAGE TODAY
THE GOSPELS
Phillips
MACMILLAN
POEMS
OF FAITH
for the
Christian Year

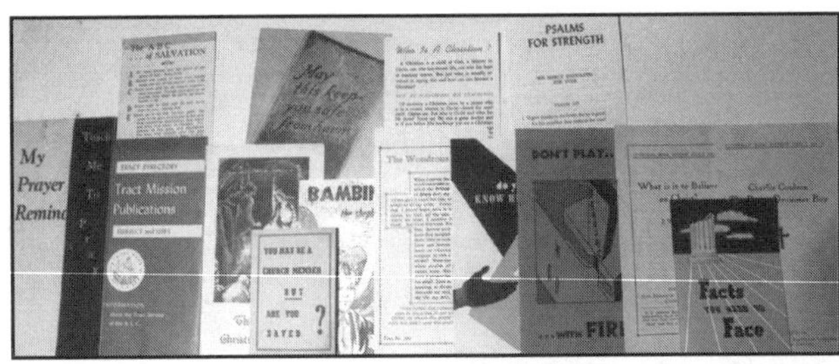
The A B C of SALVATION
May this keep you safe from harm
When Is A Christian?
PSALMS
FOR STRENGTH
My
Prayer
Remind
Tract Mission
Publications
BAMBI
The Wondrous
DON'T PLAY...
... WITH FIR
YOU MAY BE A
CHURCH MEMBER
BUT
ARE YOU
SAVED
?
Facts
Face

LITTLE
FOLKS
VOLUME 33
OCT. 24, 1954
NUMBER 43
SCHOOL
SCHOOL
SLOW

GUESS THE RIGHT WORDS
Jesus is the Son of God and the Son of Man
Jesus is both God and Man
A TEXT TO LEARN
Jesus said: "He that hath seen Me hath seen the Father." John 14:9.
A POEM

A Foretaste of the Work to Come

A Foretaste of the Work to Come

Lutheran children between the ages of comic books and Teen Magazine were considered Juniors. They weren't old enough to be a pianist for a choir, (they were just learning how to play *Jesus Lover of My Soul* using both hands—left hand F and Middle C, right hand F and A—one flat in the piece), usher for evening services (Sunday morning ushers were confirmed), help with Sunday School, have major emotional problems from reading Seventeen Magazine, drive a combine or "Make it with Wool." In other words, Juniors were just kind of little chaperoned Lutherans in waiting.

Even though the Lutheran church programs for the Juniors weren't really intense, they did give them a foretaste of the work to come. There was the Junior Choir—a real challenge with the changing voices—, the Junior League, the Junior Daughters of the Reformation, the Junior Missionary Society, Junior Bible Camp, and the Junior Confirmation program. If Confirmation was a time for memorizing, being a junior was a time for reading. There were lots of Christian books and Lutheran tracts written for this age.

Juniors helped in the church by rolling bandages for the leper colonies, playing Mary and Joseph in the Sunday School program, handling the fishpond for the Harvest Festival, and performing recital pieces—both instrumental and vocal—for the Mother-Daughter banquet. Church recreation for Juniors consisted of going on a hayride in the Fall, playing musical chairs at Junior League and

Dorcas Society during the winter*, and raking leaves for the elderly who were doctoring and feeling poorly in exchange for some lard doughnuts and a good feeling.

This is most certainly true.

** Musical chairs was usually played to "All Hail the Power...". Nine times out of ten, the pianist stopped at the 'di' in the phrase, 'bring forth the royal diadem.' Lutheran pianists never caught on, but the kids did.*

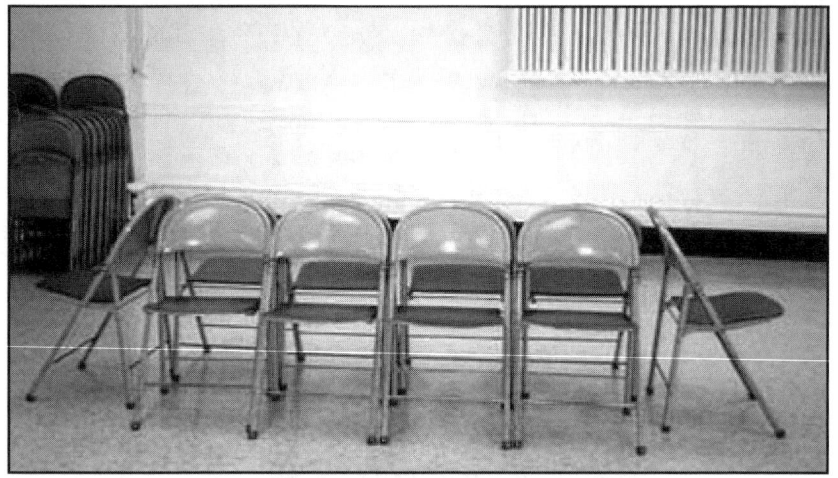

**All hail the power....
Bring forth the royal "di"...!**

Excerpts from the Bulletin

If you have a tan stormcoat that seems too snug, call Orvin Jensen. Someone got their coat mixed up with his after the *Lutefisk* Supper.

Keeping Willie Bolstad's Secret: New Year's Eve with some Lutheran "Juniors"

New Year's Eve for Lutheran kids of the 50's was often spent in two places; at home and then at church. This, of course, was for Lutheran kids who hadn't been confirmed yet and therefore could not date.

Confirmed kids, dating or not, would get together at one of the kid's homes for a party. Yes, of course, the parents were home. This wasn't even questioned. Lutheran parents knew where their kids were, who they were with, who their friends' parents were, what valley their grandfathers had come from in the Old Country, when they'd be home and which parents were hosting; i.e., which moms and dads would be serving the cocoa and pushing the teenagers' cars out of ditches. House parties were another benefit of being confirmed— along with watches, lipstick, dating, nylons, nonfarm-use driver's licenses and, if one had received enough gifts of money, luggage.

Lutheran kids who hadn't been confirmed yet stayed home with their parents and younger sisters and brothers until 11:00 p.m. They made popcorn, ate bars and leftover Christmas cookies, played Monopoly, Rook and Aggravation, and began the new jigsaw puzzle they got each year from Uncle Karl. Mom could finally let her hair down and relax now that all the holiday doings were done, the season's used Christmas paper had been ironed and put away for next year, and the relatives had gone back to Bismarck and Minot and had taken the fruitcake with them. Dad, who hadn't started to think about Spring work yet, knew this was the last night before he'd have to get out the canceled checks and the shoebox full of elevator records and repair bills, and empty the pocket calendar still holding the year-end bills. New Year's Eve was his final fling before doing taxes. The kids were excited because they'd soon be a year older and a year closer to Confirmation and to driver's permits. Everyone was in a good mood.

About 11:00 one of the neighboring parents (whose turn it was) would pick up the Junior high kids along the route. Junior High Leaguers from many directions would meet at the Lutheran church in town. At 11:30 p.m. the kids would gather in the basement to have barbecues, cocoa and bars made by a few mothers (whose turn it was). The kids, who hadn't seen each other now for almost two weeks, would tell what they got for Christmas, would whisper what their visiting cousins from the cities had taught them this time, and the girls would plan what they were going to wear "the first day back." (In 1957, the most envied was Patty who had received a "45" of Debbie Reynolds' recording of *Tammy*.)

For the Junior High Lutherans there were two things really neat about being at church that night. First, the minister didn't come, and there were very few adults around. That night, if only for a half hour, it was really their church. Secondly, a highlight of the year ending and of the year beginning would start at 11:55 p.m. and run through 12:05 a.m. For those ten minutes the kids had a real job—a real responsibility—at church! Willie Bolstad, the custodian of the church in town, let the kids in on a little secret every New Years Eve: he let the kids ring in the New Year.

Willie the Perfectionist, as the ushers called him, lived the concept that "Cleanliness is next to Godliness," even though the phrase wasn't in the Bible (which he thought it was), but really came from John Wesley, the founder of the Methodists. (Had Willie known that, his life would have been spent a little differently.) By the time the kids arrived, Willie had shoveled the walk for them and heated up the church, although in order to do so, he hadn't been able to listen to all of the 10:00 p.m. news.

Before the kids could take turns ringing, they had to listen to Willie—to his annual talk, and to the sequence of his ringing. Willie reminded the kids that clear, full, rhythmical ringing was important because Lutherans were orderly and had an image to uphold. Quality ringing was also important so that the town people wouldn't figure out their little secret. Naturally, the adult drivers and servers (whose turn it was that year) were sworn to secrecy. Those adults loved it too because they felt that for once they were part of some hanky-panky.

At 11:55 p.m. each December 31 for 16 years, the ringing began and went off flawlessly. Each year at 12:05 a.m. on January 1, the Lutheran kids—following Willie's instructions which seemed almost impossible—"shouted Happy New Year softly," and they and their Lutheran drivers went off to start a new year.

The kids going south of town begged their driver to swing past the Legion so they could see what "those kind of people" were doing. The kids just saw a lot of cars which didn't seem too exciting. As they left town, the Lutheran kids knew again that life was good, and they went home happy that they weren't like "those kind" whatever "they" were like.

All the younger Lutheran kids were safely home by 12:30. They waited up until 1:00 a.m. when the confirmed Lutheran kids came safely home so they could tease the older ones by saying something like, "You won't believe what we did and I'm not gonna tell you!" Willie Bolstad's secret was safe for another year. Of course, they didn't have to tell because all the older kids and most of the Lutheran adults in the community (whose turn it had been one time or another) had gone through it themselves. It was kind of like a Lutheran secret that no one talked about, but everyone in the community knew, sort of like when someone was p.g. and had to have a shotgun wedding.

Meanwhile, Willie "picked up the church" and then the plate of bars the kids had left for him. He took the bars home to his Mrs. who was waiting up for him (as were the parents of all the confirmed Lutheran kids). Willie asked her how the bell had sounded and she assured him no one would know the difference. As she said, "Those kids pulled off a good one this time."

Willie and his Mrs. sat down and ate the bars, happy that they weren't the kind that hung out at one. Just as Guy Lombardo burst through the radio with *Auld Lang Syne*, Willie gave his Mrs. a little peck on the cheek and wished her Happy New Year. God had been good to them that year, too.

This is most certainly true.

Twirling around basement poles is as close to dancing as many Norwegian Lutherans get.

Some kinds of cards are okay to play.

Reading for the Minister

Reading for the Minister

Six Days Ye Shall Work and on the Seventh Ye Shall Take Sermon Notes

On Sunday mornings most Confirmation classes sat together in the front pews at church to take sermon notes. In the beginning, this was as difficult as rolling a pie crust or shifting a car for the first time. However, after Confirmands got the hang of it, they were confident enough to be able to daydream and doodle a little and still turn out an acceptable set of sermon notes for the pastor.

After two years of study, Lutheran kids were ready for the real tests. For the first test most Lutheran kids were required to recite from memory all of Luther's Small Catechism—all five parts in about 15 to 20 minutes (six parts if you were Missouri Synod), but just for the pastor. Most were able to do it, but in the end, others got to say it in sections over a period of weeks.

The second test, called Catechization or Public Questioning, was open to the public. That meant parents, lonely but interested widows, and a few randoms from town came to find out if you had paid attention, learned your lessons, and could answer the $64,000 questions.

While the Confirmands stood sweating either in the front of the church or lined up and down the center aisle, the pastor grilled each one individually. For some it was just too much of a good thing and they fainted. Others just felt like throwing up. However, after it was over and all had survived, everyone—including the nervous parents who were hoping their children wouldn't blow it—was relieved.

After Public Questioning was over, Confirmands had only a few days to get ready for the Sunday Confirmation Services. While Gilman, a Confirmand, was in town to get a haircut the day before Confirmation, his mother was busy hemming his "they-sure-know-what-they-want-for-these" Confirmation suit, pressing his new white shirt and Confirmation robe, buffing his new "what-a-shame-he'll-grow-out-of-these-long-before-they-are-worn-out shoes," and putting out his new tie, socks, clean underwear, and a shaver that she hoped he would use."

Sylvia, another Confirmand, was excited about her new clothes. Finally she had a new white dress from the S & L that she couldn't wait to wear. It was a shame, she thought, that it had to be covered up with a white robe. She looked at her new Ruth Bary beige nylons she bought at Ben Franklin and hoped she wouldn't run them. She practiced walking in her new white heels so people wouldn't think it was her first pair. She couldn't wait to wear the watch that her parents had bought for her as a Confirmation gift so she could show it off to the other girls. She knew just how she was going to wear her hair, but hoped her mother wouldn't notice the pink lipstick on her lips and the light pink, almost-clear, nail polish that she had secretly bought with her rock-picking money.

That evening Sylvia watched her mom set the Jell-O and frost the "Confirmation Cake." (Her mom had given a cake decorating demonstration at Homemakers and was so good at making roses and printing frosting Bible verses that the cake looked just like it came from the town bakery). Sylvia had a hard time sleeping. She was worried that her face would break out and then, too, she was thinking about what would happen after Sunday when she knew that she could legally date Lutheran boys and wear nylons. This was as close to a debutante ball as a Lutheran girl could get.

Her mom had scrubbed, painted, and cleaned the house

for months. Furnace filters were changed, ditches on either side of the driveway were mowed, the garage door was re-hung, and manure scrapers were hosed down.

Nothing was left untouched. Now they were finally ready!

As the Confirmands were ushered up the center aisle to the front of the church, they knew that this was serious stuff. Once the pastor put his hand on Gilman's head and said, "Gilman Einar Stedje. Do you renounce the devil and all his works and all his ways?", Gilman knew the pastor was talking about teen dancing with a Catholic of the opposite sex, having a beer after barley harvest, and telling off-colored jokes in the barn. He knew he was also talking about playing poker with his friends over at Darrell's family's newly finished basement romper room and using the chips and face cards that were found behind the sauce jars which were located on the top shelf of the fruit cellar. With the pastor's hands firmly planted on Gilman's head and his parents, his sponsors, his widowed Sunday School teachers and his relatives and neighbors in the pews all waiting for Gilman to say "Yes, I renounce," he knew what he had to do. With a pang of first-time Lutheran guilt he said "yes" and knew he would just have to deal with temptations later. The other two questions, "Do you believe..." etc. were easy. Of course, he believed. He was a Lutheran after all.

After all the Confirmands had reaffirmed their Lutheran Baptismal vows by answering "yes," they partook of the Lord's Supper for the first time. The girls were more nervous about this than the boys. Most girls worried about choking on the dry wafer and coughing from the wine. Sylvia Barsness was especially nervous. Her cousin, Jean, had told her that the wine tasted like sour gooseberries right off the bush, and the pastor frowned if you made a face. Sylvia made it through it okay, though.

After the two-hour Confirmation Services, Lutheran children processed to the back of the church and shook hands with everyone, lined up for their individual and class Confirmation pictures, and then went back home with their parents. Gilman's mother quickly got out her Brownie to take a picture of Gilman with his sponsors, and of Gilman holding his Confirmation Cake. She quickly took off his carnation and put it in waxed paper in the refrigerator for safekeeping. She took the bulletin out of her purse and put it in a drawer. There it would sit until she found time to glue it into his scrapbook some day. She grabbed a good clean apron and dished up the food she had prepared for the sponsors, relatives, and close neighbors who had been invited over for dinner. *

For gifts, Confirmands usually received more money than they ever got from trapping pocket gophers, religious knick-knacks or books, a few useful Lutheran presents (see photos), and a watch from their parents.

This is most certainly true.

**After dinner, Gilman's mom said he could change out of his suit and go outside and play ball with the rest of the boys. When they got outside, Darrell, the neighbor boy, asked him if he wanted to go to the bunk house to play cards. Gilman knew he had been put "to the test" right away. He got out of it by saying that he had promised his cousins he would play ball. However, he knew that next time it wouldn't be that easy.*

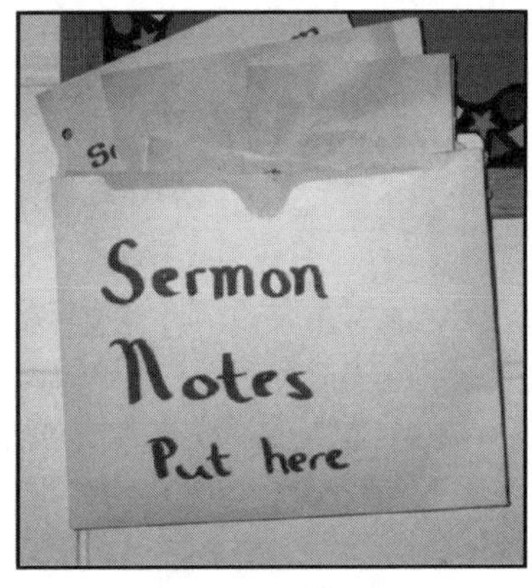

Not Much Ado about Mary

Conscientious Lutheran children spent about 540 hours* in Sunday School classes, 144 hours in Saturday morning Confirmation classes, two weeks every summer at Vacation Bible School and one week every summer at Bible Camp. This was in addition to countless hours of memory work. Yet, despite all this religious training, the only things most Lutherans learned about Mary were:

a. she was the mother of Jesus,
b. she pondered all those things in her heart, and
c. she was married to Joseph, a blue-collar guy, who worked with his hands.

Lutheran kids learned more about the three men in the fiery furnace** than about her. Lutherans knew there were three Mary's mentioned in the Bible. Mary, the mother of Jesus; Mary, the one who ticked off her sister, Martha, because she wouldn't do dishes; and Mary Magdalene, a mixed-up woman. Sometimes Lutheran kids got them all confused, and some Swedes (especially those who had gone to Gustavus Adolphus) even thought she was *Sankta Lucia.*

Lutherans didn't grow up with any visual reminders of Mary. There were no Augsburg Publishing House or standard altar pictures of her in the Lutheran churches. She was never immortalized on the "dedicated in loving memory of" beloved stained glass windows and she wasn't on bookmarkers. Lutheran kids didn't wear Mary medals, and most Lutherans only remember seeing one picture of her in their Sunday School books, the one by the manger. Lutherans had no statues of her in their churches, their homes, or in vertical bathtubs among their garden petunias and zinnias. She was never mentioned in their prayers, the Heroes of the Lutheran Faith books, flannelgraph stories or chalktalks.

Even though Lutherans had no Mary Holy Days, Mary May Days, Mary queens or Mary parades, she still seemed like kind of a holiday person to Lutherans; that is, she—just like Sivert Sivertson and his brother Sven who both set pins at the bowling alley—showed up only at Christmas time. Every Christmas Lutheran children enacted "the story."

Mary, usually played by the pastor's or the Sunday School superintendent's daughter, sat in the front of the church next to a homemade manger that a Lutheran grain farmer—who had some extra time on his hands in November of '47—had made for the annual program.

She was usually blonde and wrapped in a good used white cotton bed sheet. Her head was draped in one and a quarter yards of baby blue Dan River cotton that was bobbi-pinned to her hair. Being Mary wasn't an especially good part to have because she had no piece to say, and the other kids would tease her and tell her she was married to the awkward, lanky Knekkerud boy who stood by her, as he—under protest in his bathrobe—did his best to look like Joseph.

Even though Mary has supposedly appeared and been heard from in countries such as Portugal, Ireland, Belgium and Italy, she doesn't seem to have made any special appearances in Norway, Sweden, Denmark, Finland, Iceland, or parts of Germany since the Reformation, and she hasn't communicated one-on-one with any Lutherans since the Battle of Stikklestad.

This is most certainly true.

**1 hour for 36 Sundays a year x 15 years = 540 hours or 1 pin, 1 wreath, and 14 bars.*

***Heck, Lutherans can even spell their names. (Shadrach, Meshach and Abednego)*

The Ten Social Commandments

1. **THOU SHALT NOT DANCE FAST OR SLOW.**

2. **THOU SHALT NOT WEAR PANCAKE MAKEUP, DANGLY EARRINGS OR BRIGHT RED FINGER NAIL POLISH.**

3. **THOU SHALT NOT SHOOT POOL OR HANG AROUND THE BILLIARD HALL, GET LEWD TATTOOS OR PLAY WITH FACE CARDS.**

4. **THOU SHALT NOT SMOKE, SPIT OR CHEW (and this includes cloves).**

5. **THOU SHALT NOT CLAP, LAUGH OR CARRY ON IN CHURCH.**

6. **THOU SHALT NOT TELL BARNYARD JOKES OR POSSESS TIMM'S IMPLEMENT SHOP CALENDARS.**

7. **THOU SHALT NOT DRINK ANYTHING STRONGER THAN WHAT THE WCTU FOLKS WOULD.**

8. **THOU SHALT NOT DATE OUTSIDE THE FAITH. (Sometimes this means outside your synod.)**

9. **THOU SHALT NOT GO TO MOVIES OTHER THAN *MARTIN LUTHER* IN BLACK AND WHITE, *THE TEN COMMANDMENTS*, AND *SONG OF NORWAY*.**

10. **THOU SHALT NOT ASSOCIATE WITH ANYONE WHO COMMITS THESE THINGS.**

Getting Close to Heaven

There are three sanctioned times when Lutherans can sit in the church balcony without being talked about:

1. When the balcony is used for "overflow" at a big funeral or when there are too many people at ser–vices like at Christmas and Easter.
2. When you don't want to be conspicuous because your Richard Hudnut Cold Wave didn't take and you think you look like a haystack after a bad windstorm.
3. When you are feeling sort of like a borderline Christian because you were out too late the night before.

"Overflow" is the only guilt-free choice listed above, although those who have to sit in the balcony for overflow reasons probably got up or got going a little late. This might cause some guilt. Reasons two and three aren't guilt-free, but they are forgivable as most people have had similar experiences.

Along with the above three sanctioned reasons, there is one other use for the balcony: to keep confirmed boys as active church members. The use of the balcony by high school boys during Sunday services isn't sanctioned, but it is semi-endorsed by the leaders of the congregation because it is a way to keep confirmed youth from dropping out all together.

To split up families like this in church has been the cause of some mild controversy, but it is one area where Lutherans have tried to justify actions and compromise. As Borghild Swenson from Solem Lutheran said in 1956, "Ja, those hoodlums that sit in the balcony. But then I s'pose the balcony is as close to heaven as they'll ever get."

To supplement this arrangement, the boys of the congregation also formulated the following options for those times when the pastor is getting carried away.

Things to do in the Balcony when the Sermon is Dragging

- Spit on bald-headed people
- Play hangman on the bulletin
- Count purple-haired ladies (in times when hats aren't in style)
- Send airplanes made from the bulletins during prayers so no one will see them coming or know who did it.
- Next, try to get the paper airplanes over shafts, i.e., the walls' connecting rods
- Count bats
- Blow mouse droppings from the balcony rail onto the main floor
- Threaten to ring the bell at 11:01
- Make a list of who isn't there and make up reasons why they aren't
- Play Tic Tac Toe on the bulletin
- Figure out which bald head is shiniest
- Sing off-key on purpose
- Count the retired farmers (the ones without a cap line along the back of their heads)
- Stare at any 13-year-old girl and see if she senses it and turns around
- Try not to giggle, belch or break wind
- Be thankful you aren't a Catholic in the middle of a High Mass

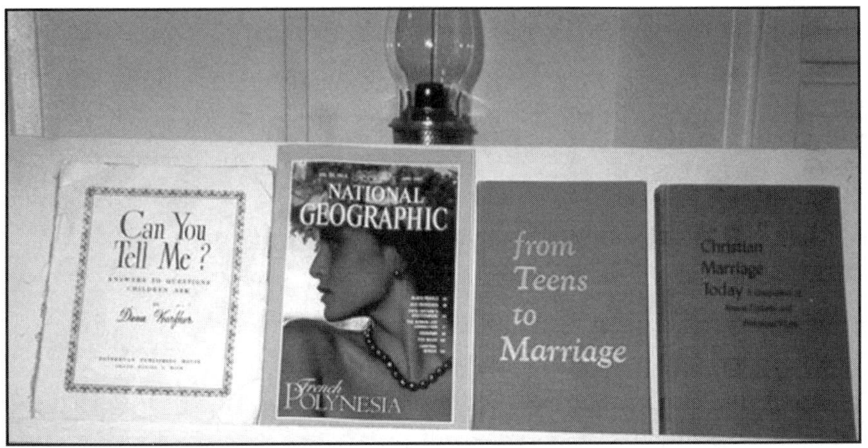

Sex ed

"Men do not marry public property."

Alvin Rogness - 1942

Gifts for boys

Gifts for girls

Kum-ba-yah

Kum-ba-yah: Puppy Love at Bible Camp

Sometime during Junior High, kids started to really discern differences—differences among ministers, kinds of Lutherans, and even between sexes. It seemed that Swedish-American Lutheran pastors were New Testament types and that Norwegian Lutheran pastors were Old Testament types. Swedish pastors smiled some, but then so did their people. Norwegian pastors took their work and life much more seriously, but then so did their congregants. At Bible Camp kids even learned about some German Lutheran pastors who had been known to show up at VFWs for wedding dances. Scandinavian Lutheran kids wondered if those German Lutheran pastors ever danced at one, but no one really knew for sure. They did know, though, that such German Lutheran pastors weren't Wisconsin Synod and figured they must be from the less conservative faction of the Missouri Synod.

Darrell Ellingson, 4-H Health King who got out of haying one year so he could go to Lilies of the Field Bible Camp, first heard about this dance thing from his bunkmate in the Leviticus Cabin. However, his bunkmate, Sherman, was from St. Cloud and Darrell wasn't sure he should believe everything a city kid said. But when Darrell told Beverly Thompson, whom he trusted because she also went to Gol Lutheran and was in his 4-H Club (piano player and historian), she said that maybe Sherman was telling the truth because someone coming from St. Cloud would sure know about other religions.

During breaks at camp, like between flag raising and

breakfast, breakfast and cabin cleanup, cleanup and morning devotions, devotions and Bible Study, Bible Study and dinner, dinner and cabin rest time, between cabin rest time (when Lutheran girls wrote letters to everyone they knew in the world) and small group discussions, discussions and beach/craft time, and between the half-hour that Lutheran camp kids had to put on dresses and dress slacks for supper and supper itself, and after supper but before evening hymnsing and vespers, and finally before 9:30 p.m. when they had to be in their cabins for devotions followed by Lights Out, Darrell and Beverly spent a lot of time discussing German Lutherans and other heavy things.

By Wednesday, Mail Call didn't even seem exciting to Darrell and Bev. That night they even volunteered for K.P. so that some other kids could finish crafts. By Thursday night they were sitting together in chapel and at supper, the one meal when they didn't have to sit in cabin groups.

Although the theme for the week was based on Amos, Darrell and Bev began to understand the Book of Ruth better. "Thy people shall be my people" took on a strong significance by Thursday. Bev and Dare (as she fondly began to call him) seemed destined for each other because they shared the same people and the same God already. They wouldn't have to deal with that whole "whither thou goest" moving away mess. Like Bev said to Marlene Olson, her bunkmate in Rose of Sharon Cabin who was also from Gol Lutheran but a year younger, "My oh my, the Lord does work in mysterious ways. I've known Dare for 15 years and his farm borders our pasture. I never dreamed something like this could happen."

On Thursday afternoon, the day of the greased watermelon contest, a bunch of kids asked Jim, the lifeguard, if they *had* to have their bunkmates for buddies in the Buddy System. Jim, having guarded two groups of campers for two weeks already, and having been a lifeguard at

Lilies of the Field the summer before, knew what was up. Besides, he had been a camper himself once. "Just pick someone you can trust your life with," he said. Irrespective of gender, new configurations of Buddy Tags hung on the same nail for the next two days. Naturally, Bev and Darrell—numbers 73 and 31—paired up, she in her strapped, rubber bathing cap, and he with his noseplugs.

On Friday before beach and kittenball time, Darrell took Beverly to the canteen where he bought her a charm for her bracelet. It was the Martin Luther rose symbol just like the one on their Sunday School pins and on the cover of their First Year Confirmation Book. In gratitude, Bev bought him a strawberry ice cream cone and they shared a Hires Root Beer.

Friday evening was the traditional Closing Program Talent Show. After the camp octet sang and the camp band played, (1 cornet, 8 clarinets, 1 sax, 2 baritones and 1 accordion), Bev played Ole Bull's *Sæterjenten's Søndag* . As Darrell turned the pages for her he looked out at the campers. It sure looked different than it did on Sunday night when the group first met in the Chapel. Sunday night the girls sat on the south side and the boys were north of the aisle, town kids showing off in the front pews of their respective sides, and farm kids acting decently towards the back. Tonight there were boys intermingled with girls, and town kids with farm kids.

Darrell spotted a few couples that he knew just wouldn't make it, especially farm girls paired up with city boys. Even though the couples ritualistically traded addresses Saturday morning and wrote in each others' autograph books, Darrell had learned some stuff about city boys from Sherman. He had said that by the time the boys had unpacked at home Saturday afternoon, they had thrown the addresses away and gone to see their real girlfriends. Sherman said they would tell their real girlfriends that the girls at camp were a bunch of nice girls who sewed their own clothes, but they were nothing to write home about. To Darrell, *Sæterjenten's Søndag* had never sounded so nice. He flipped a page, looked at Bev's charm bracelet, smiled and felt happy all over.

The highlight of the week at camp was the traditional last-night-at-camp campfire down by the lake dubbed Galilee. After the Certificates of Attendance (published by Augsburg Publishing House) had been handed out by the cabin counselors, the final hymnsing began and some of the guy counselors and Jim, the lifeguard, rowed a boat out into the middle of the lake. After the campers had sung *He Lives, Onward Christian Soldiers, This is My Father's World* and *Abide with Me* for the last time, and the light from the bonfire was almost out, the guys in the boat lit a wooden cross that had been dowsed with gasoline. While it burned, the campers sang and then hummed *Kum-ba-yah* which was led by the visiting missionary stationed in Madagascar who had taught it to them.

The bullies even behaved for once, a few town girls cried, and no one noticed the swarms of mosquitoes. Promises were made to meet at the County Fair in August and at the League Convention at LBI in October. As Bev took it all in, a shiver ran down her back. She looked at Dare and said, "Now I know why the camp brochure said, 'bring a light-weight jacket.' The air conditioning really does come right from the lake!" Dare slid a little closer and put his arm around her—to keep her warm.

Finally Pastor Dale, a New Testament type, thanked the group for being such an outstanding bunch of well-rounded, decent youth; thanked them for the week, invited them back next year, and gave a closing prayer. He told the kids they could be out until 11:00 that night, and urged them to leave the bonfire silently and to reflect upon the week and the burning cross.

Once up the hill toward the main camp, the volume picked up some. The "singles" of both sexes organized their last snipe hunt and took off in the woods with flashlights. The couples hung around the red pop-bottle machine, the bell tower, the tetherball pole and behind the dining hall and chapel.

At 10:59 p.m. Bev made it into her cabin. (She was a farm girl so she wasn't bawling.) Besides, she'd see Dare every day including Saturdays at Confirmation class and Sundays at services. Marlene, who was sitting in her shorty pajamas on the top bunk, whispered to her, "Did he kiss you? Did he?" and Bev just glowed and said, "None of your bees wax."

Bev fell asleep thinking about the $15.00 for tuition she had worked for all year and decided that her first real investment had really paid off. Marlene didn't sleep at all. She tossed and turned trying to figure out if Lutherans were reading Ecclesiastes selectively—"a time to dance, a time to embrace, and a time to keep silent". Silence she understood, but she started to wonder about all the camper couples and the embrace stuff. She wondered about Beverly's soul. Then she started to wonder about the souls of everyone she had ever known who had died. Were they saved? Did they go to heaven? How does one know if they are saved? Bible camp is a soul-searching time for Lutheran kids.

Saturday, following an early noon meal dubbed The Last Supper by the staff, and after being constantly reminded by counselors, pastors, missionaries, and parents to not forget bathing suits and washcloths on the line, the kids departed Lilies of the Field Bible Camp.

Sophomore year was a wonderful year for Beverly and Darrell and they didn't miss a day of school, or one event at church. After Christmas he gave her his ring and she wore it around her neck. The following June, Darrell had to stay home and help with the haying as his older brother, David, had been drafted. Beverly left for a week at Bible Camp again. During the week she was gone,

Darrell met another decent Lutheran farm girl from a neighboring school at 4-H Achievement Day, and Beverly finally took that guy from Paynesville up on his Coke offer from the year before and, when he went home, he didn't throw her address away for a long time.

This is most certainly true.

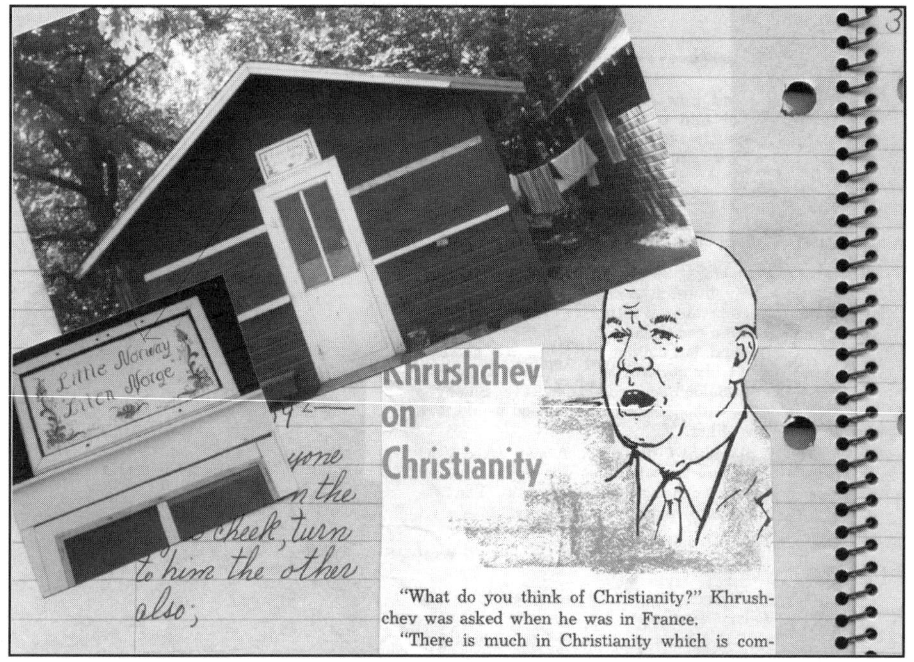

Little Norway
Liten Norge
cheek, turn
to him the other
also;
on
Christianity
"What do you think of Christianity?" Khrushchev was asked when he was in France.
"There is much in Christianity which is com-

Excerpt from Camp Brochure

There will be some mosquitoes but as a precaution, the grounds have been sprayed with DDT.

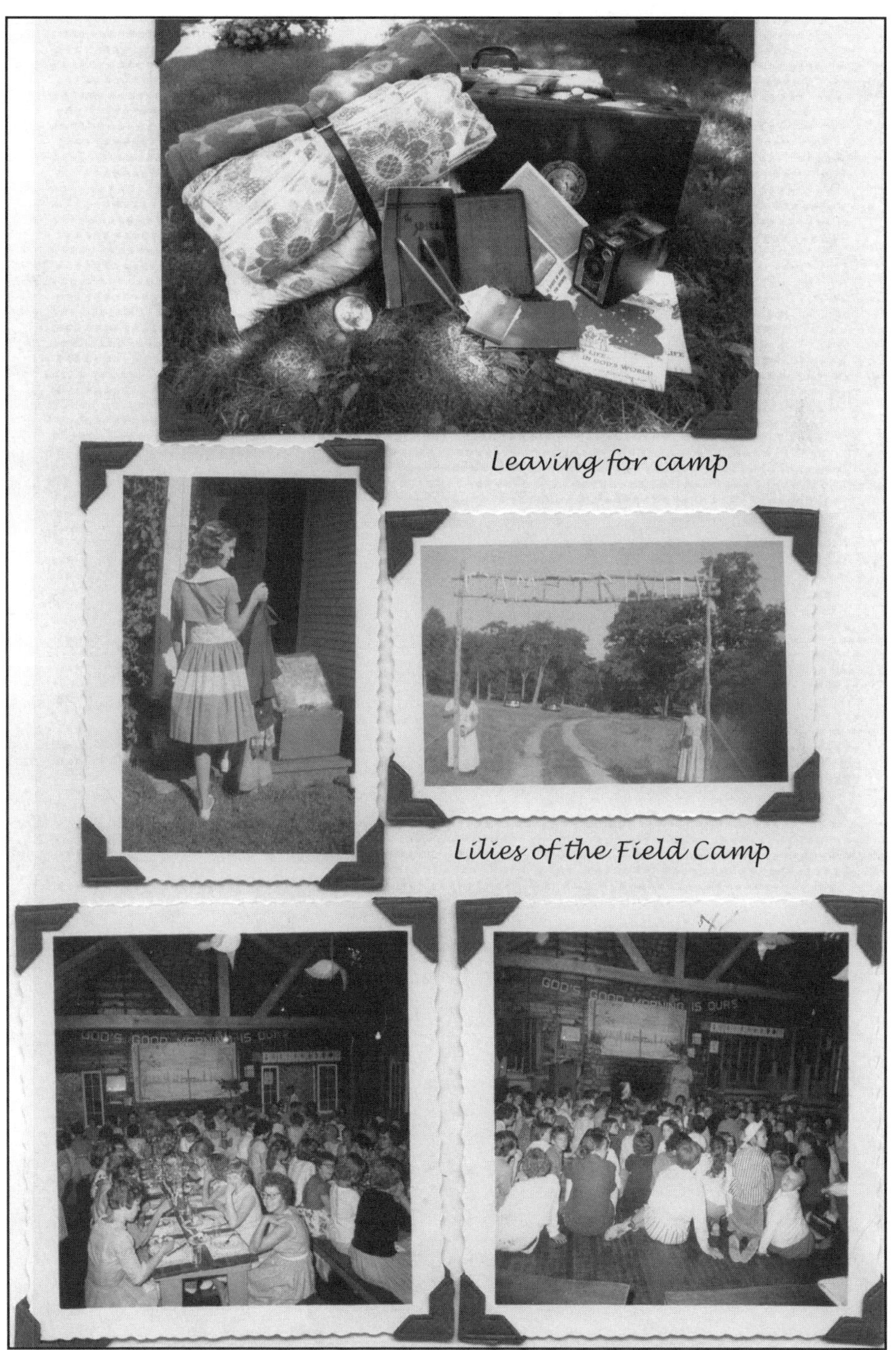

Leaving for camp

Lilies of the Field Camp

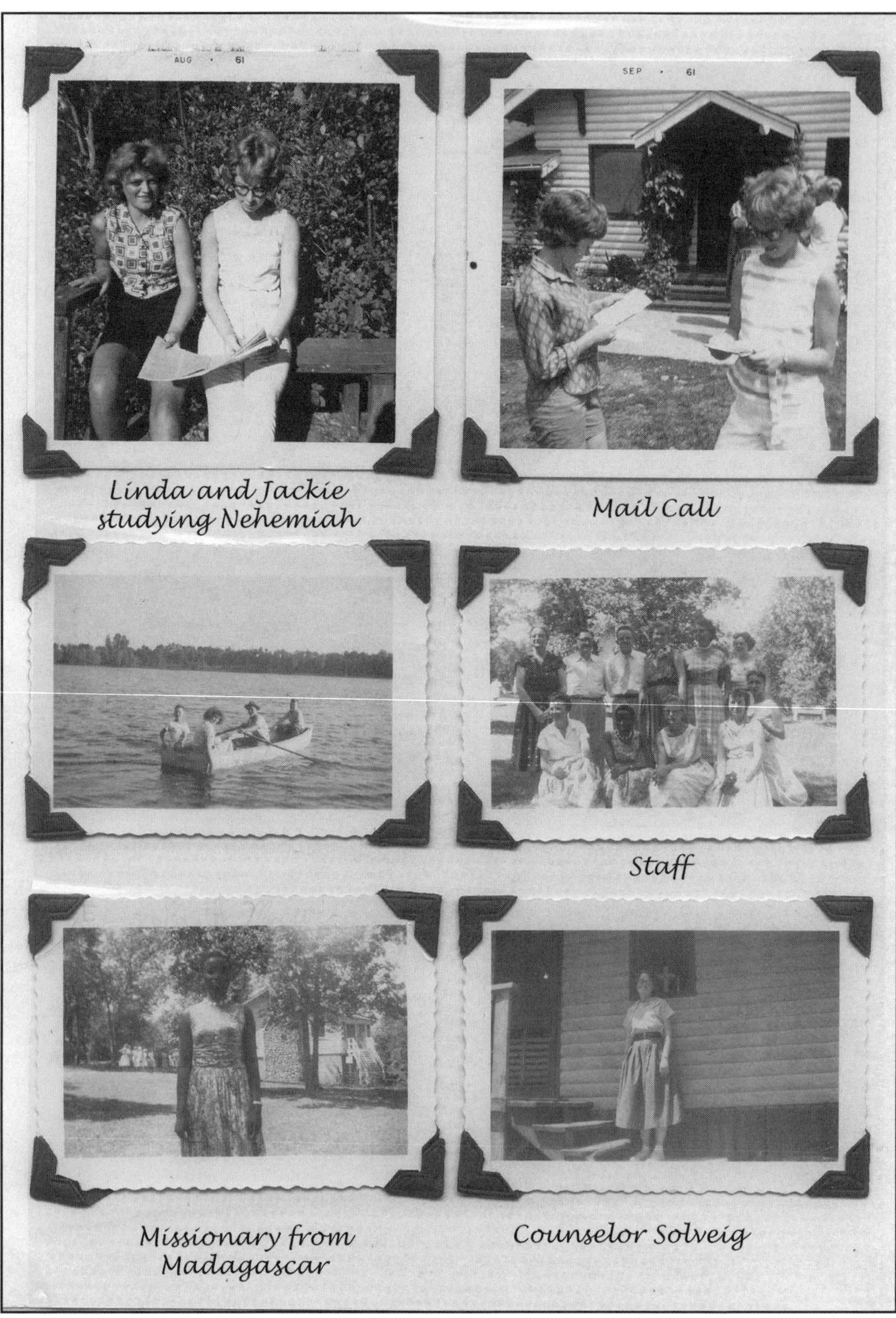

Linda and Jackie studying Nehemiah

Mail Call

Staff

Missionary from Madagascar

Counselor Solveig

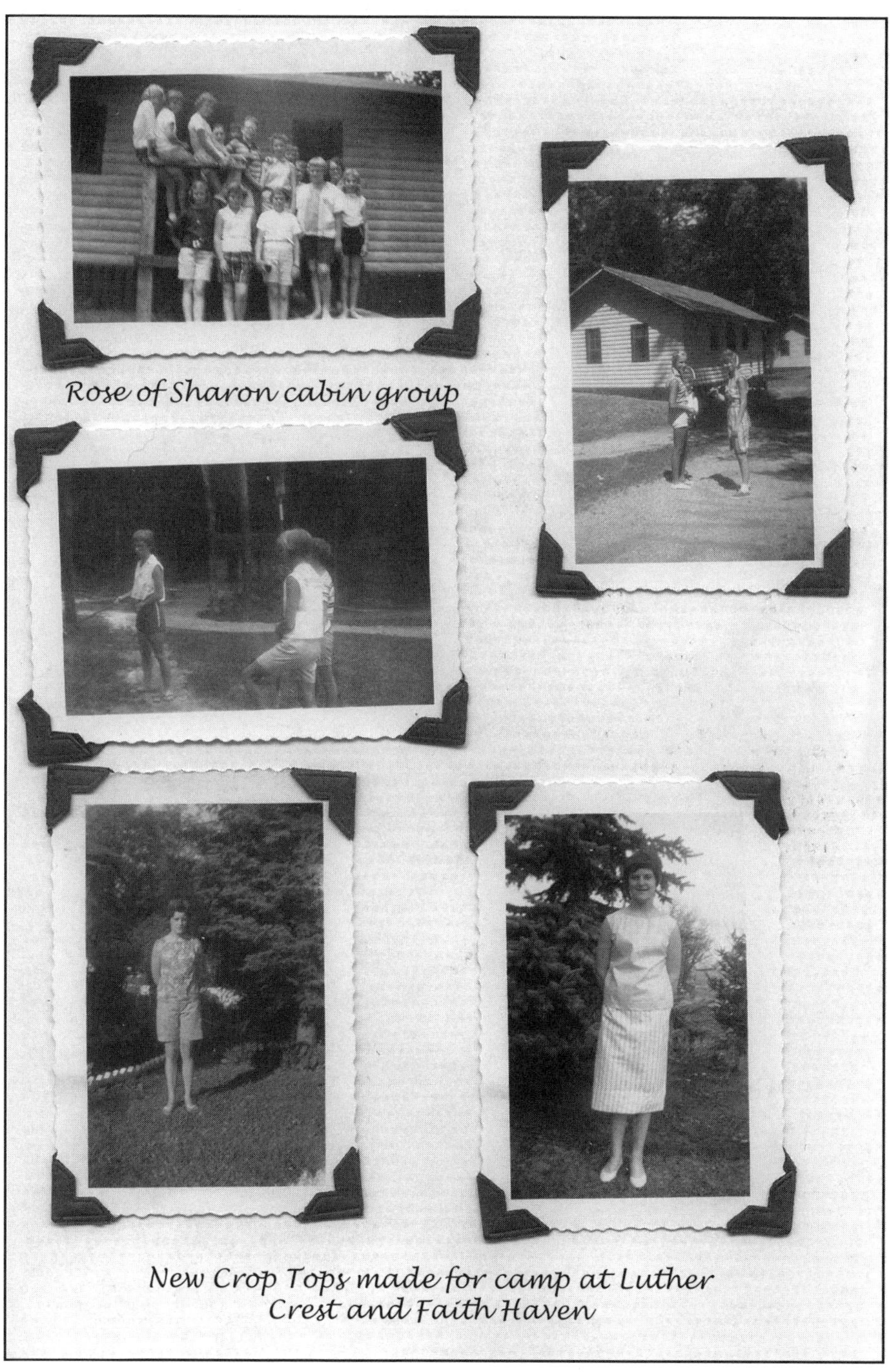

Rose of Sharon cabin group

New Crop Tops made for camp at Luther Crest and Faith Haven

Marlene & Bev
in bunks

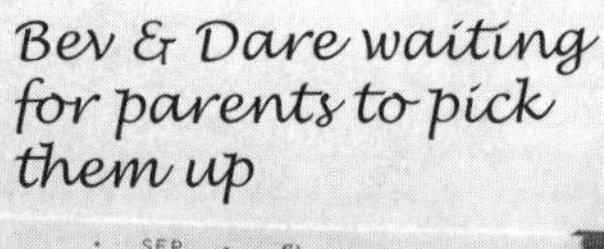
Bev & Dare waiting
for parents to pick
them up

UNOFFICIAL CAMP SONG

I like Martin Luther,
Good old Martin Luther,
Played in the Reformation
Band.

Ninety-five theses,
Knocked the Pope to
Pieces,
I think Martin Luther's
Grand.

See You Soon in Saskatoon: or

San Francisco	'55
Missoula	'58
Miami	'61
Detroit	'64
Seattle and Dallas	'67
New York	'70

See You Soon in Saskatoon

See You Soon in the Church Basement:

With rock and roll music coming out of AM transistor radios, American Bandstand on black and white television, and "they have no shame at all" things going on in the secular scene, the Lutheran churches knew that if they were going to keep the youth interested in the church after they were confirmed they had to offer them some good, wholesome, clean Christian fun and fellowship. The Lutheran church recognized from early on that the youth needed to be with their own kind.

Earlier Lutheran youth organizations, like the Daughters of the Reformation, the various Missionary Societies, Young People's Society and Youth Choirs all involved more study and work than play. Although Lutheran theology deems work much more important than idle play, the Lutheran hierarchy succumbed to society's pressure and organized doings for their youth that were part study, part work and part play. So the local Leagues (Walther or Luther, depending upon the church you belonged to); regional youth gatherings in places like Des Moines, Fargo, Sioux Falls, Omaha and Alexandria; and the "See You Soon in Saskatoon" national conventions usually held in sin cities became the Lutheran church's answer to the pressures of the secular society.

After Confirmation most Lutheran students belonged to Walther or Senior Luther League. This was usually held weekly in the church. Even though there were no parents in attendance, the pastor was there. But, it was the youth officers who called the meetings to order, read the minutes of the last meeting and gave the treasurer's report. There was rarely any old business, and new business consisted of picking delegates and handing out sign-up sheets for regional gatherings. However, if it was a national convention year, there was a lot of both old and new business to discuss.

The youth gave the devotions that their mom's had prepared, lead the short Bible studies and read the canned prayers. Peppier-than-the-old-hymnal songs were sung from the new Let's Sing Youth Songbook. The meeting adjourned after an offering and the singing of *We Give Thee But Thine Own.*

Lunch was either cookies and nectar for a regular meeting, or barbecues, pickles, cake and cocoa for when the youth went on their annual Fall hayride or winter toboggan ride. Sometimes Lutheran youth from other Lutheran churches in town would be invited to the hayride and toboggan parties.

At Christmas time the youth went caroling to the shut-ins. At Easter they served the Easter breakfast. If they needed to fundraise for a national convention they also had an Easter car wash.

Secular activities in the church included shuffleboard, blowing marshmallows across the table, and the questionable, flirtatious, sometimes frowned-upon game of Wink 'em, wherein a Christian Lutheran teenaged boy would stand at the back of a chair where a Christian Lutheran youth of the opposite sex was sitting. The object of the game was to grab the girl and hold her to the chair when the Christian Lutheran teenaged boy in the center of the circle signaled the girl to run for the center by winking at her. Lutheran girls were nervous that nobody would wink at them and Lutheran boys were excited, but nervous about where to grab a Lutheran girl. If he grabbed her at the neck she could choke, and if he grabbed her farther down and had secretly taken a shine to her, he would have broken his Confirmation vow of renouncing the devil and all his works and all his ways. As Widow Snustad had said to Pastor Borgrud after hearing about this, "No wonder some of them become p.g. Is there no shame in the Lutheran church any more?"

Another game sometimes played at Valentines was a shoe mixer. The Lutheran girls put one of their shoes in a pile and a blindfolded Lutheran boy would grab a shoe out of the pile and then eat a boxed lunch with the girl whose shoe he had grabbed. In other words, it was a Lutheran Blind Date. Sometimes it worked out girl-wise and lunch-wise, but often it didn't. Widow Snustad didn't approve of this game either. As she said to Pastor Borgrud, "What in the world are we teaching them, anyway?"

League protocol didn't vary much from one Lutheran church to the next.

This is most certainly true.

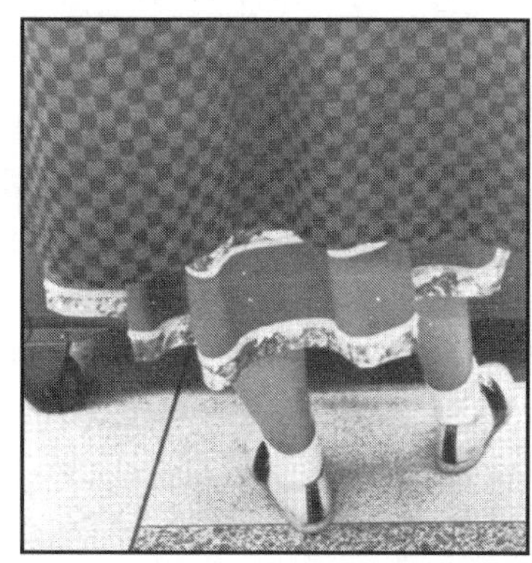

Waiting in line for cocoa

Parish League Party 1954

Blowing marshmallows

See You Soon in Des Moines

Some Lutheran youth - especially the active ones - attended regional youth gatherings. These were usually more fun than the weekly League meetings, but didn't hold a candle to the national conventions. These gatherings were usually held in a big neighboring church or high school gym on a Saturday or Sunday afternoon. Usually two young delegates, the pastor and other interested Lutherans from each church in the general area attended.

There were several sessions to attend, and it was at these sessions that Lutheran youth got a chance to actually meet Lutheran youth from neighboring towns whom they had only seen at rival basketball games and at Bible Camp.

The youth from the larger towns intimidated the youth from the rural congregations. Big town youth knew how to play tennis and golf and just seemed more worldly. Usually they were the ones who were elected regional officers, even though the rural girls knew shorthand and felt they could handle the secretary's job just as well as the girls from the larger towns.

It didn't seem to matter that the rural girls had planned what they were going to wear and planned what they were going to say; they just didn't quite cut the mustard. Lutheran rural boys rarely attended regional gatherings because they had to do barnchores and were too busy, literally, picking mustard.

Group singing, which was often accompanied by a teenaged girl from a larger town who could sight read anything that was requested from the diverse youth that were in attendance, was more exhilarating than any singing they had heard in their local church. Usually the lunch was better too.

This is most certainly true.

See You Soon in Saskatoon...or Missoula, Miami, etc.

Six times between the years of 1955 and 1970, thousands of confirmed Luther Leaguers from across the nation boarded buses, trains and automobiles and gathered together for national conventions in large cities. Luther League Conventions were held in San Francisco in '55, Missoula in '58, Miami in '61, Detroit in '64, in both Seattle and Dallas in '67 and in New York in '70. Before '55, it was "See you Soon in Saskatoon."*

There were many a hoop a Luther Leaguer had to jump through to get to a convention, but the first hoop was the most difficult. For a Lutheran kid to convince his Lutheran farmer dad who had gone through the Depression that it was necessary to go 2,000 miles away from home to become a better Christian was no easy task. Gingerly mentioning that all the other Luther Leaguers at church were going didn't work. Neither did the "I promise to pay you back" line. However, in the end, the Lutheran kids usually won out and got to go, but not before getting the "I never ever want to hear you moan and groan about rock picking, throwing down silage, cleaning the pig pen or shoveling barley ever ever again. And you too, Miss, you're not going to lie in bed Saturday morning and think the world owes you a living." And the sermon continued, "I've worked all my life and kept my nose to the grindstone. The only place your mother and I have been was to Gooseberry Falls and that was 23 years ago and it certainly didn't cost what this trip is going to set me back. In my day, it was Depression time you know, and we were just thankful to have food on the table. You know, nothing's good enough for kids nowadays. But this is it. Do you hear me?'

We heard him all right, but the guilt didn't settle in yet. After months of preparation, fundraising, planning and packing, Lutheran kids were off to a big city that they had never seen before; a city they had only read about in geography class.

As they were boarding the buses and trains, Lutheran kids got one more sermon from their parents about safety, paying attention, and foolishly spending money. This was for their own good, they were told.

The rides were long, but fun. Car after car after car of recently confirmed, agreeable, Rook-playing, wholesome Luther Leaguers on a train was what Paul must have been envisioning when he told the Corinthians that there should be no dissension among them, but that they should be united in the same mind and the same judgment.

The Norwegian Lutheran farm kids from the prairie were seeing so many new things on their trip that their heads were just swimming. Palm trees, mountains and oceans, just to name a few. A bit of Lutheran guilt crept into a few Luther Leaguers as they thought about their toiling parents back home who had never really seen anything at all.

After the trains and buses were unloaded and the Lutheran kids were checked into their hotels and had their convention packets and name tags, they went to their first required meeting in the counselor's room to go over all the rules and regulations and to make sure they understood everything.

Even though there was going to be a little free time between meetings at the Convention Center, the counselors let them know that the main purpose of this trip was spiritual, not recreational, and that all Luther Leaguers were expected to be in attendance at all sessions. Of course everyone agreed and made it to all the sessions the first two days. Just walking with thousands of Lutherans into a Convention Hall that was twenty times bigger than any winter show auditorium they had ever been in, made an impact. But after two days of meetings and sessions,

Luther Leaguers not only knew the theme of the week - Jesus is Lord, Christ is Living, We are a Peculiar People etc., but felt comfortable going back to their hotel by themselves.

By the third day, most Luther Leaguers had rationalized that if they had spent all this hard-earned money to get to this convention, they shouldn't waste the opportunity to see some sights around the city. Who knows if they would ever get back this way again or not. So off they went—to baseball games, restaurants, sunbathing by the ocean, shopping at department stores bigger than they had ever seen, and touring areas of the city they had been warned to stay away from. These were things they didn't write home about, but sure enjoyed.

After four days, most of the Luther Leaguers were running short of spending money and knew they were heading home in a couple of days. The ride home was long and not as harmonious as the ride to the convention.

Besides most Luther Leaguers were thinking about their dads working in the fields and their moms canning in the kitchen, and the fact that they had wasted good money on seashells, cowboy hats, umbrellas, Space Needle trinkets and baseball paraphernalia.

The next Sunday in church Luther Leaguers gave their reports to the whole congregation. Some were better reports than others. Everyone talked about the interesting speakers and how much they had learned. They talked about the impact of hearing thousands of Lutherans raise their voices in song, singing such songs as *On Our Way Rejoicing.* However, nobody mentioned free time until during the questions and answer period, Widow Snustad said, "And what did you do in your free time, then?"

This is most certainly true.

**As of today Lutheran youth are still attending national conventions. The City of New Orleans, where sin is visible on street corners, was the site of the 1997 convention. Even though reports are in that the Luther Leaguers were well behaved, it is a well known fact that there were dances held every night at the Convention Hall. (It's a blessing that Widow Snustad has been called home, then.)*

Walther Delegates to Des Moines

Midwesterners arriving in Miami

Fram Fram, Kristmenn Krossmenn

Fram Fram, Kristmenn Krossmenn

After high school, many Lutherans continued their education by taking Bible correspondence classes, going to Bible School, attending a Lutheran College and/or a Lutheran Seminary. These higher education institutions were training grounds for future generations of Sunday School and release time teachers, Parish Education Workers, choir members, organists and Pastors.

These institutions were financially supported by the church and successful alumni. However, some of the colleges and seminaries became just too liberal for you-can-always-count-on-them alumni Lutherans like Widow Snustad. As she told the president of the Concordia C-400 Club, "I don't give money so the devil can dance."

Fram Fram through the Mail:

Christian correspondence courses could be ordered through places such as The Lutheran Bible Institute (1619 Portland Avenue, Minneapolis 4, Minnesota); The Moody Bible Institute—earlier known as the Chicago Evangelization Society—(153 Institute Place, Chicago, Illinois); and Augsburg Publishing (425 Portland Avenue South, Minneapolis 15, Minnesota). Lutheran Women, who had been educated at Normal Schools and were called upon to teach Sunday School, Release Time and Home Bible Studies, used these correspondence courses as their guides.

Widow Snustad subscribed to them to make sure the material remained on the up and up.

This is most certainly true.

Fram Fram from Portland Ave, Mpls. 4, Minn:

There were several Bible Schools located across the nation that Lutheran students attended. The most well-known were the Lutheran Bible Institute, (or LBI as it was commonly called) in Minneapolis and Seattle, the California Lutheran Bible School in California, and the Moody Bible Institute in Chicago.* Later on, after a series of mergers and changing hymnals, the Medicine Lake Bible School of the Association of Free Lutheran Congregations in Medicine Lake, MN was added to the list. When a Lutheran in the 50's graduated from high school, the Depression was over so they had more choices than (as Widow Snustad said) was deemed necessary. They got married, joined the military or went to Bible School, Business School, Ag School, Repair School -- Auto and Appliances, Electrician School, Secretarial School, Beauty School, Deaconess School, Nursing School, or College. Some found a job, and others farmed or helped out on the homeplace.

Lutherans who went to Bible School usually spent two years living in dorms learning about the Bible, the Lutheran Faith, and actively looking for a life long helpmeet. Some of them were there trying to figure out if they should really be a parish worker, minister or missionary. Others were there because everyone else in their family had gone there, some were just sent there. Some students hadn't quite figured out why they were there. Lutherans who went to Bible School were usually decent and didn't rock the boat.

This is most certainly true.

**The Moody Bible Institute and the Billy Graham Evangelical Association were not Lutheran, but were embraced by Lutherans because they seemed decent enough, kind of like the "Give-Me-That-Old-Time-Religion" Haugean brand of Lutheranism.*

A room full of Ylvisaker wanna-bes

1st semester finals

Lutheran girls pretending they go to the U

Lutherans understand that cleanliness is next to godliness

Fram Fram for Four Years

Not all Lutheran high school graduates went to Lutheran colleges, and not all Lutheran colleges had just Lutherans enrolled in their schools. However, it was a safe bet that most students at Gustavus Adolphus and at any school called Augustana had ancestors from Sweden, and those at St. Olaf, Luther, and Augsburg had ancestors from Norway. Those who went to Dana could tell you the colors of the Danish Flag, those at Suomi knew a few Finnish words and how to take a sauna, and those who attended one of the numerous Lutheran colleges called Concordia had tasted sauerkraut more than once. The only exception was Concordia College in Moorhead. Those students ate Cream Peas rolled up in their *lefse* even though they were called Cobbers.

Lutherans attending a Lutheran college in the 50's and 60's did not have to prepare themselves for any big culture shock. Some of them even shared the same last name—but were not related. No one knew how to dance or play Bridge. No one could tell you what kind of hard liquor was in a Martini, but most all of them knew what commandment contained the words "Betray, Belie and Backbite."

Lutheran parents sent their kids to Lutheran schools because, just like at home, there were rules to follow. There were mandatory curfew times set for the girls and no boys were allowed in the girl's dorm rooms except at the college's annual Christmas open house and then only if a book was placed in the doorway to keep it from shutting. (Many Lutherans used match books for this purpose). All students were expected to attend chapel daily and to be dressed up in church clothes if they were going to eat in the school cafeteria on Sunday. (A lot of Lutheran students went hungry on Sundays. This is most certainly true.)

Most of the students of the 50's and early 60's knew their parents wanted them to find a good Lutheran boy or girl at college. That meant they should find someone who was decent, God-fearing, modest, sensible, thrifty, and knew how to work hard. As Widow Snustad told her son Harold in '54 as he was putting his grip on the bus to go to Augsburg, "Stick to the girls at Augsburg or LBI. There is so much *thrash* in Minneapolis you could end up with almost anything."

When Lutheran parents paid "good hard-earned money" to send their kids to a church college, they expected their kids to study hard, get a job, join the choir, and make something of themselves. However, things got tough after the red hymnal was introduced into the Lutheran church. Everything fell apart.

Lutheran colleges across the nation had their hands full and their Chapels empty. Students were organizing petition drives for legalized dancing on campus and everything else that smacked of Moral Decay.

Kids were trying to find themselves and like Sven Ole Nestergaard said as boldly as he could to the president of St. Olaf College, "Now think about it. How can my boy get lost? He's only 150 miles from home. Good night, then!"

Lutheran kids started to question everything, and Lutheran colleges buckled under the pressure and gave in to demanding students.

---

*One year in the middle 60's, four St. Olaf students and one long-haired hippie-type professor who wore sandals without socks, had a goatee, didn't go to Chapel and got his way paid for free, went on a J-Term to York, the old Viking dig, in England.

They were going to study "Peas and Their Impact on Early Viking Life as it relates to Twentieth Century Norwegian Lutheran Church Basement Recipes." Two of the students, Ole Nelson and Nels Olson (not related) were Pre-med turned Philosophy majors, one Forrest Adams Hill III was a Pre-law turned Political Science major, and one Einar Ingram Johnson wanted to major in Economics but he didn't have the nerve to declare his major because his dad, Wallace, had warned him many times that 1) "Anything without a practical application is a waste of everyone's time and money," 2) "If you are going to take classes on 'The Theories of . . .' you might as well go to Vo-Tech and take something real," 3) "Work doesn't count unless it hurts," 4) "You're only as good as you can work and just look at all the worthless bankers who only work part-time and think it's normal," 5) "You don't have all your life to sit up on that hill and dream about things you can't change anyway," and 6) "If you get too uppity in your thinking, I'll take you down to Sheldahl's and you can see firsthand for yourself what real work is all about."

Einar Ingram Johnson had lots to think about, but he was relieved the J-term was in January, the time of year his dad would be sitting at the dining room table with his shoeboxes full of tax receipts grumbling about the U.S. Government and preoccupied with what was in front of his nose.

So, on the fourth of January, the four students and the hippie professor who skipped chapel motored to the Wold-Chamberlain Field in Minneapolis and boarded the airplane bound for England. Einar Johnson was both as nervous and as excited as he could get. He had never seen the ocean before, much less from an airplane. His mother, Bernice, who hadn't been right since she got to waltz with Lawrence Welk, had initialed all his underwear and told him to beware of wolves in sheep's clothing, keep some money in his shoes, and always wear a scarf around his neck because she had read in some magazine (she couldn't remember which one) about a lady who nearly died from the constant mist that they have in England which can chill a person to the bone.

Ole Nelson and Nels Olson, the two Pre-med turned Philosophy majors who both came from the suburbs, both had grandpas who had RR addresses, both had uncles who were Missionaries overseas, and both had great-grandpas who came from Norway, also were excited. They had both tried out for the St. Olaf Choir and neither had made it, but they didn't have to feel guilty because their parents hadn't made it either. They decided this was the next best thing for a chance at seeing some different territory.

Forrest Adam Hill III was neither excited nor nervous. He was from Out East. His parents, who didn't have a drop of Norwegian blood in them, were divorced. Neither of them had a clue who the choir director at St. Olaf was, much less where Northfield was located. His mother, Charlotte Hestor, an active member of the Daughters of the American Revolution, read a brochure that Forrest had received in the mail from St. Olaf because he had a high ACT score, and she thought it might be a place that was homey and quaint because they served homemade rolls. She thought: This is the place for Forrest—a kid who is having a tough time. She signed him up both for her sake and his. Forrest had been to England many times so he was just going for a lack of better things to do.

As soon as the plane landed in London, the hippie professor who skipped chapel told the boys he had his own research to do so he would see them in four weeks. The four students were left to fend for themselves. Forrest knew his way around so the rest just followed him. Einar Ingram Johnson had never seen so many people and such a variety in his entire life. Ole Nelson and Nels Olson, the two who didn't make choir, had both been to Oslo but found London to be more enticing and exciting. The next day the four students were supposed to go to York to start the research but Forrest, the one from Out East, suggested they detour to Liverpool to see the Beatle's first stomping ground. All of them agreed. Einar Ingram Johnson thought: Why not, you only live once. After a couple days in Liverpool, they made it to York.

In York they got so sidetracked with the pubs, the nightlife, and everything else that wasn't going on in Northfield that they just didn't get down to business to do their research. After living like prodigal sons for three and one-half weeks, they headed back to London to meet up with their hippie professor who skipped chapel. In the train on the way down to London, they brainstormed between pints about how they could write their research. Ole Nelson and Nels Olson from the suburbs thought they could just look up peas and Vikings in encyclopedias and pull something together on the weekend they got back. But Forrest Adam Hill III had a better idea. He said, for a small fee, he knew a guy Out East who would write the whole thing. They were all relieved, but Einar Ingram Johnson was feeling some Norwegian guilt for wasting good time and good money. How could he reconcile *Fram Fram, Kristmenn, Krossmenn* with having someone else do all his work? But Einar Ingram Johnson was an innovative thinker and this is why he knew he should be in economics. He thought to himself, I'll just get some County Extension Bulletins about Peas and add a little of my own thoughts and this way, it won't be all wrong.

He also knew he'd feel better when he went home to visit and show his slides, and his mom, the chair of the local Welk Fan Club, would make him some cream peas on toast.

This is most certainly true.

**The story of the four St. Olaf students—the latter portion of the section on four-year schools—is taken from Cream Peas on Toast: Comfort Food for Norwegian Lutheran Farm Kids (and Others) by Janet Letnes Martin and Suzann Nelson. Caragana Press, 1994.*

Arriving in a suit, but driving on the Quad anyway

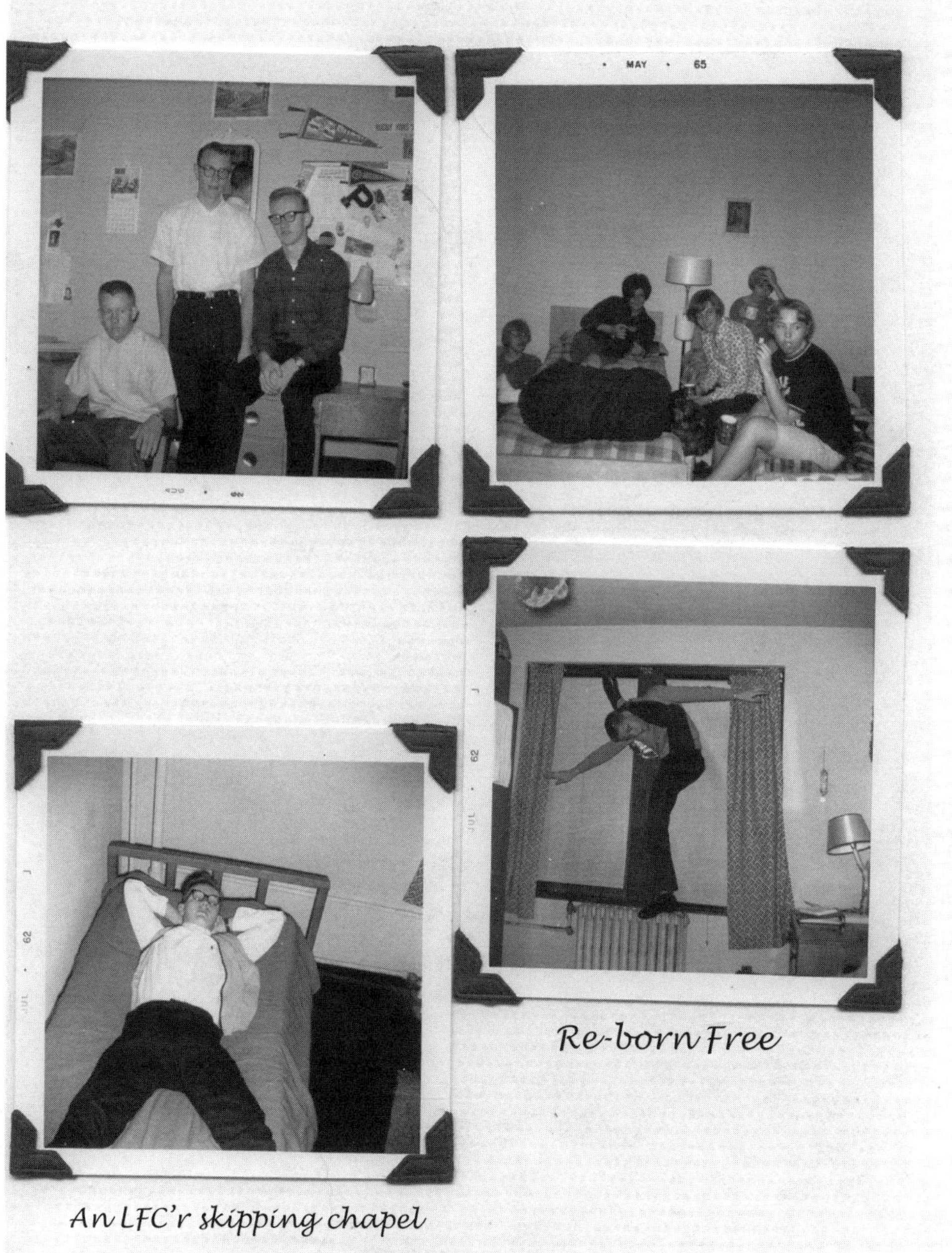

Re-born Free

An LFC'r skipping chapel

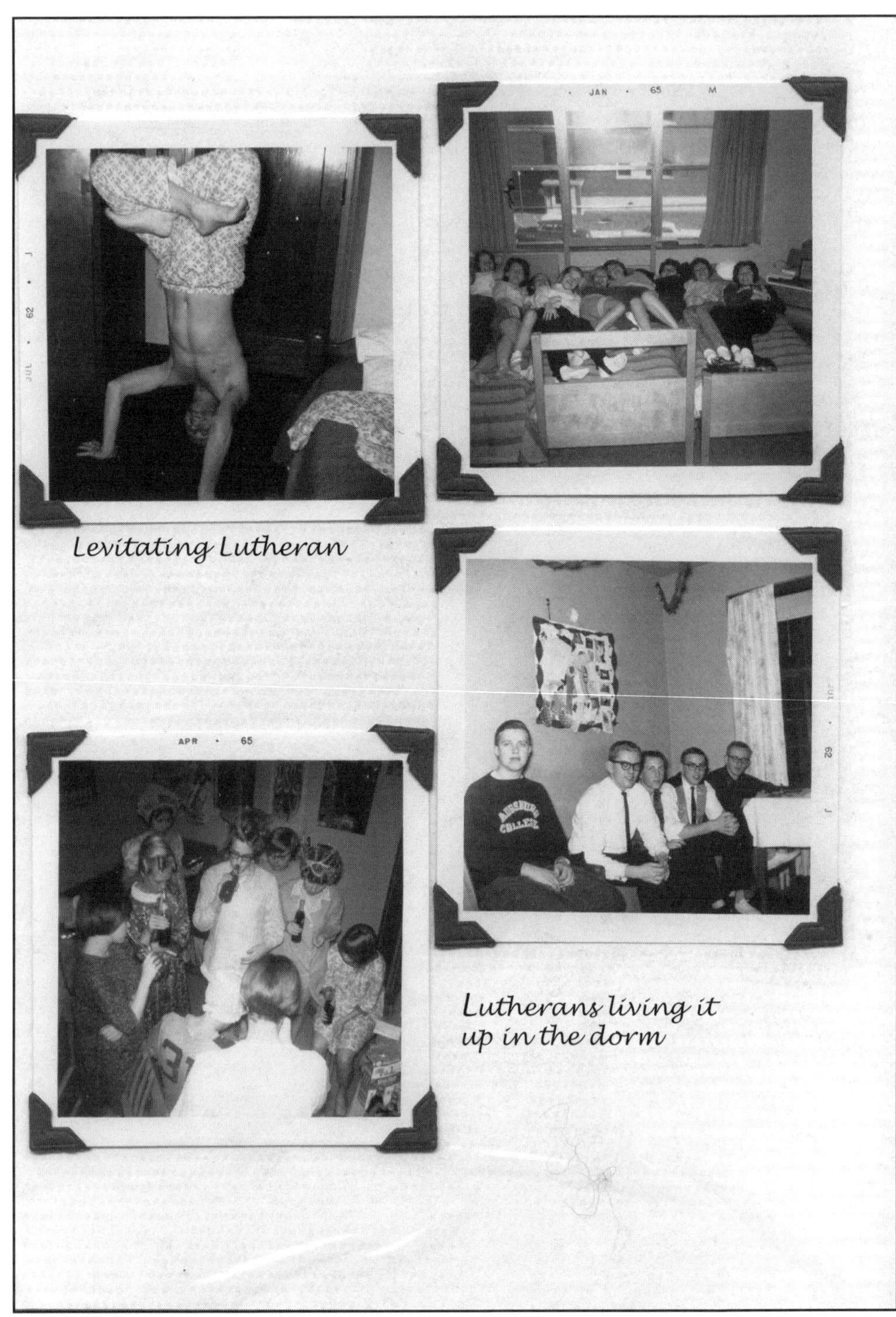

Levitating Lutheran

Lutherans living it up in the dorm

A Letter From Home

Sunday Afternoon

Dear Carol Ann,

I just got a letter off to your sister, and now I'll do yours before your dad gets up from his nap and I have to get him his coffee. It has rained for four days straight. As they say, when it rains, it pours. It sure has been a lazy day. I wonder when it will ever let up. Are you studying hard? I hope so. It's a crime what one has to pay for education these days. Did you enjoy those Brown Betty bars I sent? I sure hope so with the price of postage. It costs more to mail them than what it did to bake them. What a fright. And then Ole, Jr. said Maria was sending a card to the Pope. I told him that was a complete waste. I got the recipe from Olga H. Her sister had sent it from California, and Olga is going to put it in the new church cookbook. And then they say that postage is going up. I wonder where it will all end.

Church was half empty today. I've saved all the newspapers for you from September. I'm sending them back with Vern Jensen's son who attends that vocational school down there. I'm also sending your boots and mittens and that scarf that Aunt Elsie gave you last Christmas. I hunted high and low for that scarf and finally found it in the south room. The way things are going we're sure to have winter before Thanksgiving. Even though we pray for the harvest, we continue to hoe. It will be a race to get the corn out. Maybe you could take the bus over to his dorm and pick those things up. He's driving all the way out here to the farm to get them and I don't want to bother him too much. Kind of a quiet kid. He seems nice. He was home for his uncle's funeral. And you can't guess who else was there? Maria. Hugging and touching people she barely knew. She bawled so much she embarrassed everyone including the pastor. Have you ever heard the beat of it? And Ole, Jr. just sits there and thinks she's cute. I wonder what he ever saw in her anyway. There was more there at the funeral than I thought would show up. We thought that we would run out of food, but we didn't. We even had *enough left over for supper at home. Your dad didn't go. He doesn't like funerals, you know, so he only goes to the ones that he has to.*

Do you remember that Severson girl who graduated a couple of years before you—the one whose parents live out north of town about 3 miles? I heard at the funeral that she is pregnant by that no good lazy Peterson boy. He couldn't hold down a job if he wanted to, and his dad sits up at the liquor store every night. I couldn't remember her too well so I looked her picture up in the annual. You wouldn't believe what it says under her picture. "With blushing face and twinkling eyes, some-day she will take the prize." Well, she sure did—getting that Peterson kid! I feel sorry for her, but she made her own bed, and now she will have to make the best of it. Her sister was no different.

Well, no more news around here. I have to get a letter off to Verona. Study hard and prove yourself. You know your dad isn't convinced that it is necessary to send girls to college. He says money doesn't grow on trees. But I told him it isn't enough in this day and age to be good—you must be good for something.

Love, Mom

Monday a.m. I forgot to tell you that John Johnson had a stroke. I heard that he died last night. I'll write about it next week.

This story taken from Second Helpings of Cream and Bread by Janet Letnes Martin and Allen Todnem. Redbird Productions, 1986.

For Better or for Worse

For Better or for Worse

Thou Shalt Not Turn

Whether you were a Lutheran or a Catholic parent, your whole world was turned upside down when your kids married outside the faith.

It was called "Turning," and it had to do with guilt.

When Luther Martin Walther married Margaret Mary McCarthy, Inez Walther knew without a doubt she had failed, and her German Lutheran son was headed straight for hell. It didn't help Inez either when Widow Snustad told her, "You're just going to have to hold your ground and knock some sense into that boy. Anyone who would sign over his kids to the Pope, get married in the morning and agree to a wild wedding dance at the local VFW Hall has certainly given up his inheritance in the Kingdom."

Even though Inez believed that her son, Luther Martin, knew better and would have to answer to God himself someday, she worried about how her future grandchildren would turn out. It broke her heart to think about kneeling "little Walthers" dabbing themselves with holy water, crossing themselves as they prayed to statues of dead saints and not being in the Sunday School Christmas Program. Widow Snustad told her, "You'll just have to get a copy of Egermeier's Bible Stories and read to them every chance you get."

The McCarthy Family wasn't any happier than the Walther family about this arrangement. They had sent Margaret Mary to parochial school for 12 years and then she went and fell in love with one of those arrogant, way-ward "publics" who had never once darkened the door of a confessional booth or experienced any remorse or guilt for missing Sunday obligation. As Francis McCarthy said to his wife, Theresa Rose, after hearing the news, "Jesus,

Mary, Joseph, what did those nuns teach her anyway! She won't even be able to have a decent mass marrying a Lutheran. She might as well just go down to the court-house because it's not going to count anyway."

But Mary and Luther felt differently. Mary secretly admired the fact that Luther could just sit down and eat a cheeseburger on Friday, and not only not have any of that "you're going to get struck dead" Catholic guilt if you don't confess this and say three Hail Marys, but he never once had to bare his soul publicly in church to anyone, ever!

Luther, on the other hand, didn't understand "how this was done," but it was kind of an exciting thought to think that he could play cards and bingo in church, go to dances, shoot pool, drink a beer, and then erase all that type of Lutheran guilt in a ten-minute session with Father O'Malley in a curtained booth.

No amount of pleading from either family worked. Luther Martin Walther and Margaret Mary McCarthy were married at noon (which is somewhere between Catholic and Lutheran times) on Saturday, May 17th in Our Lady of the Prairie Holy Catholic Church. Only a few of Luther's relatives showed up, and several of them "finished the Lord's Prayer." The reception and dance was held at the VFW where lilacs bedecked the tables. Walther's parents left before the dance and right after the cake and coffee.

As expected, Widow Snustad didn't show up, but Willie Bolstad, who always knew that the Walther kid was decent, not only showed up but stayed and two-stepped with his wife.

This is most certainly true.

(If you are interested in reading any more about the way things were for Catholics and Lutherans, read They Glorified Mary, We Glorified Rice by Janet Letnes Martin and Suzann Nelson, Caragana Press, 1994.)

A Lutheran Proposal:

"Say, how'd ya like to be buried in the family plot, then?"
Oliver Johnson

Area girl to plight her troth

Mr. and Mrs. Chester P. Johnson proudly announce the betrothal and forthcoming marriage of their daughter, Olive Ruth, to Mr. Oliver J. Johnson of this community. No date has been set for the wedding.
This is most certainly true.

Useful, practical, Lutheran shower gifts

Svea Lutheran to Host Town's first ever Golden Wedding Anniversary

A 50th wedding anniversary for Mr. and Mrs. Hjalmar Lundeen will be fittingly observed Sunday afternoon in the Svea Swedish Lutheran Church basement. The doings, to be hosted by the grandchildren, will commence at 2:00 p.m.

When asked what their secret was for 50 years of wedded bliss, Mrs. Lundeen said, *"hela vagen gaar han med mig."** Mr. Lundeen said, "Oh, we just keep busy and don't let *ingenting* bother us."

All of their living children, grandchildren and great-great grandchildren will be in attendance. One son, Karl, who had served his country well, was called home last year.

The general public is invited and lunch will be served.

As the honored couple are both counted among the cherished ones in this community, a collection is being taken up and Mrs. Lundeen will be presented with a purse of money to be used as she so chooses. Mr. Lundeen is to be presented with an ebony cane handcarved in Dalarna with an engraved handle that states, *"Jäg er svensk."*

This is most certainly true.

**(He goes with me the whole way.)*

Gratulerer med dagen!

And Emma poured

From the Social Scene

MISS OLIVE JOHNSON FETED AT BRIDAL SHOWER

On Sunday afternoon, September 3rd, the Nordlund Lutheran Church Parlor was the scene of a gay pre-nuptial Miscellaneous Shower given in honor of Miss Olive Johnson. This was a joint effort lovingly given by her high school and normal school friends.

The program opened with devotions from I Timothy 3:1-5, and prayer by Ione Agrimson, local parish worker and friend of the bride. The church's talented trio—Misses Melinda Larson, Elaine Grosnick, and Connie Ackerson—treated all in attendance by beautifully singing a peppy tune entitled "I Met My Little Hubby Then Down by the Riverside." They were accompanied by Miss Sarah Bacon.

Miss Judy Anderson, this community's first grade teacher, gave a cute little reading entitled: "In order to be fulfilled, you have to bargain your way through life."

Misses Ann Larson and JoAnne Sylvester were in charge of the fun games. A game called "What do you REALLY know about our bride?" was especially enjoyed by all. Misses Janice Thompson and JoAnne Digree were in charge of decorations, including making the clever chore boy and measuring spoon corsage. Miss Ellen Larson was gracious enough to take several snapshots and promised to send everyone in attendance a picture of this momentous occasion. Miss Susan Garner was in charge of door prizes and went overboard to make sure everyone received a special memento.

Miss Diane Grund was in charge of gifts, and Miss Margaret Engel had the duty of recording the gifts and folding up the wrapping paper and bows. Normal school friends, Misses Mary Timm and Sandra Pagel, were in charge of making the sumptuous dainty lunch, and Miss Janet Nord was in charge of the punch bowl. Misses Suzann Johnson and Janet Letnes made mints in the yellow and blue color scheme that had been selected by Miss Olive Johnson for her nuptials.

Miss Olive Johnson thanked everyone profusely for the lovely gifts and for making this such an unforgettable experience. She invited them all for a Christmas luncheon at her house where she promised to serve *lefse* made on the new Bethany *Lefse* Grill she received from the committee as a gift. Other useful and generous gifts that Olive received, and which will come in handy when she takes up housekeeping, included a clothes hamper, a red Westclox for the kitchen wall, a kitchen step stool, a decaled metal garbage can with a flip-top and foot petal, and a collapsible ironing board with pad and cover. A good time was had by all.

This is most certainly true.

OLIVE JOHNSON KEEPS SAME NAME AFTER NUPTIAL VOWS

A wedding of local interest took place at half after three on September 19th at rural Nordland Lutheran church when Miss Olive Ruth Johnson, eldest daughter of Mr. and Mrs. Chester P. Johnson became the bride of Mr. Oliver J. Johnson son of Mr. and Mr. Johnny B. Johnson of Grandrud Township. The impressive double-ring ceremony was solemnized by the Reverend B. J. Tjornholm.

The church organist, Mrs. B. J. Tjornholm, played a medley of prenuptial and wedding music. Mrs. Ingvald Berg sang *O Promise Me* before the service, accompanied by Mrs. Tjornholm on the piano. As the radiant bride came down the aisle on her father's arm, Mrs. B. J. Tjornholm played the traditional wedding march at the pipe organ.

She was met at the altar by the groom and his attendant. Miss Bernice Oftadahl, friend of the bride sang *O Perfect Love*, accompanied by Miss Stella Engvold at the piano. As the bridal couple knelt at the altar, Mr. Walter Johnson, cousin of the groom, sang *The Lord's Prayer,* accompanied by Mrs. B. J. Tjornholm at the organ.

The church altar was banked with ferns and decorated with lighted tapers in candelabras and baskets of yellow and white gladioli and white mums.

The center aisle of the church was marked by burning tapers and lilies in tall standards.

The lovely bride was bedecked in a white satin gown fashioned with fitted bodice and an overskirt of net trimmed with lace and a jewelry neckline. Seed pearls adorned the leg o' mutton sleeves. Her fingertip veil of illusion fell from a coronet of pleated net trimmed in seed pearls. She wore a single stand of pearls which was a gift from the groom. Her only other jewelry was a wristwatch. For something old, she carried her grandmother's white lace hanky. She carried a lavish bouquet of white carnations, baby mums and stephanotis entwined with ivy.

Her sister, Miss Lorraine Johnson, was her only attendant. She was gowned in a short-sleeved powder blue and yellow ninon over taffeta formal with a sweetheart neckline. She wore elbow length dress gloves and headdress. She wore matching earrings, a gift from the bride. She carried a small bouquet of pale yellow carnations and blue stock. Miss Carol Ann Johnson, niece of the bride, was the flower girl. She was very sweet in a floor length dress of white dotted Swiss which had a sash of grosgrain ribbon. She carried a basket of colored sweetpeas which she sprinkled in the path of the bride.

The groom wore a dark brown suit with a white carnation boutonniere. His brother, Duane Johnson, the only groomsman, wore a standard dark suit and white carnation boutonniere. The ushers, Warren Johnson and Elroy Johnson, wore white carnations.

The bride's mother wore a street length black dress of sheer over taffeta with accessories to match. She wore a shoulder corsage of feathered yellow carnations with greenery and matching satin ribbon.

The groom's mother wore a two-toned brown and tan two-piece serge dress with a shoulder corsage of Esther Reid Daisies with greenery and satin ribbon with accessories to match.

The bride's grandmother wore a navy blue two-piece alpaca trimmed afternoon dress complemented by a shoulder corsage of bachelor buttons and white button mums with black accessories. The groom's grandmother wore a powder blue two-piece light wool suit with matching accessories and a shoulder corsage of white feathered carnations.

The reception for the happy couple was given in the church parlors immediately after the ceremony. The prettily appointed bride's table was centered with a three-tiered fruitcake covered with white icing and topped with a miniature bride and groom. The cake was made by Mavis Johnson, cousin of the bride, from Winger. Lighted candelabras, yellow and blue crepe-paper streamers and garden variety flowers completed the motif.

The guests were served a sumptuous wedding lunch. Mesdames Harold Johnson and Lester Johnson poured. Mesdames Wayne Johnson and Lawrence Johnson cut the cake. Mesdames Ole Tingvald, Lars Nyhaugen, Morris Prestholdt and Hjalmer Fretheim were in charge of refreshments. They were assisted by Mrs. Milton Evavold, Mrs. Hans Thronson, and Mrs. Wilbur Benson. Mrs. Norvald Nelson, (nee Betty Bakken), of Mentor, Minnesota and formerly of this community, was in charge of the guest book. Assisting with the gifts were Mrs. Irwin Soholt and Mrs. Hank Alhaug.

The waitresses all received, as gifts from the bride, white organza aprons with heart-shaped pockets which the bride had fashioned and sewn. The waitresses were Misses: Margaret Goderstad, Eileen Helmstetter, Patricia Todnem, Myrna Gulsvig, Virginia Syltie, Lana Bothum, Darlene Meyers, Janice Differt and Nancy Lovas.

After the reception the happy couple left immediately in their Packard for Itasca and other points of interest in Northern Minnesota. For going away the bride donned a soldier-blue coat trimmed with squirrel over a gray gabardine suit. Her corsage was of white carnations centered with a yellow mum. Black accessories accompanied her traveling ensemble. On their return home, they will take up housekeeping on the groom's homeplace where he is engaged in farming.

The bride is a popular young lady of this community, having graduated from Fertile High School and Moorhead Normal School. The groom's sunny disposition and knack of making friends make him a general favorite.

May happiness attend them.

Attending from a distance were Mr. and Mrs. Ted T. Johnson of Moorhead, Mr. and Mrs. Donn J. Johnson from Fergus Falls and Misses Margaret Goderstad and Patricia Todnem of Minneapolis.

This is most certainly true.

Reflections on Silver

Right up there with Reformation Sunday stood the Silver Wedding Anniversary! This was a celebration for long-standing members of the congregation who had been married only once and to the same person for twenty-five years. It was a time for uncles, aunts, cousins, and friends to rejoice in the church basement on a Sunday afternoon.

The children "put on" the celebration, but the real work was done by the ladies of the Aid who painstakingly arranged the details well in advance of the day. The cake was usually a bakery cake, second to none, with silver bells and the number 25 glistening on top. The corsages matched the trim on the frosting and the mints. Open-faced sandwiches (usually egg salad or minced ham), Jell-O, bars, pickles, and punch made for a good afternoon lunch.

The Mr. hated to be there. This was his time to nap. Besides, all this fussing made him feel a little foolish. But the Mrs. loved it! It was her time to shine! After all, she had brought many pans of bars for other silver celebrations, and to think that her children all "turned out!" Sometimes the Mrs. even wore her wedding dress for the grand occasion. If, after six children and all those years she could still squeeze into it (that is, with

the help of her good girdle), she was entitled to wear it. Usually, though, she just bought herself a new dress and got a new permanent for the pictures.

The program was the highlight—at least for the adults! Songs were sung and stories were told. Many of the stories had been heard time and time again, but everyone laughed and clapped heartily anyway. The grandchildren played their piano pieces. And there were the readings! Those were the clever little poems, essays, and stories on marriage found in farm periodicals, The Lutheran Herald, and Ideals.

For the kids, the nuts and mints made the day. Outside of weddings which they rarely got to attend, silver wedding anniversaries were the only time they had free access to them. And other than an occasional dirty look from the lady pouring coffee at the end of the table, it was clear sailing! The nuts and mints were wiped clean before the coffee pots were passed around for the second time. Then the kids started on the sugar lumps.

And, oh my, the gifts! There were silver trays and silver bowls, and all those crisp new dollar bills tucked in the cards. How could they ever thank everyone the Mrs. commented as the Kodaks were snapping.

When it was over, the Aid cleaned up the kitchen, took home the dishtowels to wash, and were out of the church by

5:00 p.m. They had to get home to start supper. Besides, the men had chores to do.

This is most certainly true.

**This story is taken from Cream and Bread by Janet Letnes Martin and Allen Todnem. Redbird Productions, 1984.*

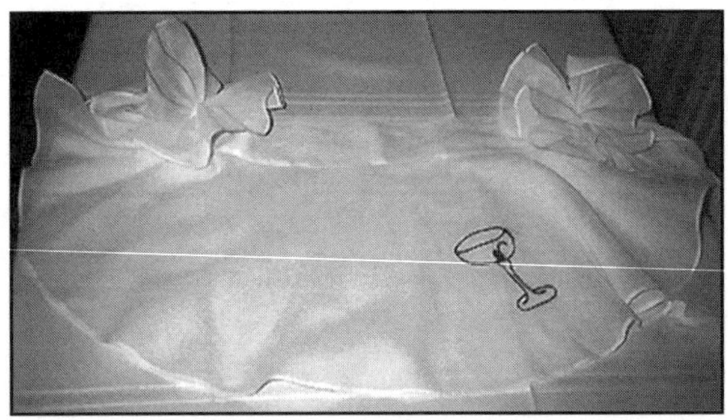

Thou Shalt not Turn!

He is not Gone, he is only Away

He is not Gone, he is only Away

Local man buried in rites at Cresco

Emil Mortensen, one of the oldest settlers of this township, died unexpectedly at 8:00 o'clock a.m. Sunday morning, September 4.

Mr. Mortensen was born outside of Roskilde, Denmark April 6, 1893 and came to this country with his parents when he was two years old, settling in Howard County. The farm which they homesteaded was his home for over 60 years where he endured all the hardships of the early settlers. The farm is now operated by Karl and Martin Refsdal.

Mr. Mortensen was a blacksmith in Decorah before he was united in marriage in 1928 to Florence Hansen, who proceeded him in death. They were the parents of 13 children, nine of whom Mr. Mortensen leaves behind to mourn his passing. The nine offspring who survive are as follows: Curtis of Fergus Falls, Minnesota; Arthur of Story City, Iowa; Delbert and Albert of Decorah; Phillip and Leonard of Ames, Clarence who farms the homeplace; and daughters Norma of Caledonia, Minnesota and Dagny Elwoodsen of Cresco. Since his beloved wife's passing three years ago, Mr. Mortensen has made his home with the Elwoodsens with intermittent visits to the Bethany Home for the Aged in Decorah, but never for an extended period. Thus, it was with great surprise that his daughter found him deceased this past Sunday as she tried to awaken him for services.

In addition to his children and grandchildren and numerous nieces and nephews, he leaves behind a host of friends and neighbors who will deeply mourn his loss.

Funeral services will be held at 2:00 o'clock on Wednesday at the Aalborg Danish Lutheran Church outside Cresco where he had been a faithful member for many years and had held many important offices. He was well pleased to leave this world and enter into the promised kingdom on the other side of the river of death. Arrangements are being handled by the Andersen Funeral Home. Interment will be will be made in the Aalborg Cemetery.

Excerpt from the Cresco Register—Posten

Mr. Mortensen was one of those good persons who never offended anyone, always nice to deal with in every respect, and straight, honest and upright as any human being could be, and we do not believe we are saying too much when we say that for a person of his disposition, it would be impossible to have any but friends, and he could make others happy by his always smiling disposition. We, with his many fond acquaintances, extend our most heartfelt sympathy to the bereaved family. May their tears soon cease to flow.

Expressive Lutheran Funeral Statements

Oh, he looks so natural.
Doesn't she look nice?
It was such a big funeral.
He's earned a good rest.
She was called home so suddenly.
I hope I go in my sleep.
He won't have to suffer anymore.
The Lord giveth and the Lord taketh away.
I think she was about my age.
They did such a nice job on him.
Ja, it sure went fast with him.
Sure thought she'd make it through Christmas.
She looks so peaceful, no more worries.
It's good she went so quickly.
Ja, thanks for the lunch then.

The Eidfjord Lutheran Cemetery Board as Usual

When Alfred Engelstad called the Annual Meeting of the Eidfjord Lutheran Cemetery Board to order at 7:30 p.m., four other board members were there, as usual. Holger Hjelle, the youngest on the board, was absent, as usual.

Holger had so many other things going on that he hardly ever did anything for the Board. But, as Bardolph Skrefsrud reminded the group annually, Holger had been appointed to serve because some younger blood was needed and, of all the families in the township, the Hjelles had the most relatives buried at the Eidfjord Cemetery. Therefore, it was only fair and proper that Holger Hjelle had been appointed to serve, even though he wasn't the best board member in the world. After the usual grumbling about the younger generation and about Holger's shiftless behavior, 74-year-old Alfred Engelstad began with the first matter of business and called for elections.

Adolph Skrefsrud, nominated Bardolph for secretary; Bardolph, Adolph's twin brother (both aged 78), nominated Adolph for treasurer, and Marvin Rustad—hoping that Alfred would never have to miss a meeting—nominated Oscar Lang for vice president, as usual. Seeing as how this was the year when the president's position was up, Oscar Lang then nominated Alfred for president again. Alfred, who once told the pastor that he felt being Cemetery Board president was his "calling", had served in this capacity for 11 three-year terms, right through his hip surgery. Most folks around there thought it made good sense that Alfred should be president again because he kept the papers at his home, and he lived closest to the cemetery so he could keep an eye on things. Besides, he always kept his Sunday suit in the car ready to be emergency pall bearer at the drop of a hat. All nominations were seconded and passed, as usual.

Other than location of the farm, there were two other ways to keep being president: self-nomination and stacked nomination. Alfred had only nominated himself twice; once when the Skrefsrud Twins' cows had gotten out so they didn't get to the meeting until after the election (but still before lunch), and the other time had been so long ago that Alfred couldn't remember the circumstances.

Regarding the stacked nomination business, Alfred had long ago learned how far one of his wife's Sour Cream Pies would go. The Skrefsrud Twins were, like they themselves said, " bachelors who had never married." They still lived together on the homeplace where they had been born, and thought those pies were just about as good as fruitcake. With Bardolph's and Adolph's votes, along with his own, Alfred could count on being reelected. Of course, sometimes Alfred kind of wondered what would happen if Holger ever showed up, but then that's why Alfred always scheduled the Annual Meeting for the same night as the first game of the district basketball tournaments. Holger's son, Earl, was co-captain, but he was also a senior so Alfred knew he'd have to schedule future meetings when Holger would be busy with something else. Maybe it could be later in the Spring when planting was in full swing. (All the other Board members were semiretired, having cattle only and renting their cropland out to Holger.)

With the most important item of business out of the way, Alfred moved on to lesser agenda matters:

1) What would they do if the Swede's side (the part of the cemetery located on the south side of the church) filled up before the Norwegian's side on the north? Oscar pointed out that this was a real possibility because "most of the Norvegians live to be 84 to 97 years old, on averch". Bardolph said, "Well, even though prices keep going up and up, the Swedes will just have to start a cemetery of

their own." Adolph said, "Well, we aren't going to let them be buried on the north side. I couldn't rest peacefully with them by my side". Marvin Rustad, who wasn't an officer and was the second youngest on the Board said, "On the other hand, they couldn't live together in life so maybe they can in death. It might be a start." Sometimes he got a little too liberal for the others, but he was real good at reading aerial maps of the cemetery. No action was taken on this issue, as usual.

2) Did they have to keep mowing where "the suicides" were, and how long should they keep burying them outside the fence? Now that there were fewer bums, should "the suicides" be buried in the transients' section—at the back of the cemetery, but inside the fence?

Bardolph, expressing the views of some of the area's Norwegian Lutherans said, "Well, they're dead. I suppose it doesn't matter much to them, then." His twin brother, Adolph, said, "Ja, I suppose it's bound to happen sooner or later. It's just too bad the back is the prettiest part of the cemetery with all those lilacs and stuff." Oscar said, "You yust never know. Maybe dere'll be another Depression and da bums vill come back." Marvin the Liberal said, "Maybe we should just bury them with their families like we do with everyone else." No action was taken on this issue, as usual.

3) What should be done about mowing now that the Happy-Go-Lucky 4-H Club, after 20 years, had decided to give up this community service and get jobs at the Piggly Wiggly and lumber yard in town instead? If they had to hire a man with a machine-mower, would they have to put a moratorium on plastic geraniums?

Bardolph said, "Ja, that younger generation. They're for the birds. What happened to their willing hands and hearts and heads?" Adolph, the board treasurer asked, "Can we get the women to do it?" Oscar, the analytical one said, "It sure vould be a lot easier to get somevun to mow if dose diggers in the 30's vould hafe meshered so the rows between the grafes were efen." Throwing in his two cents worth, Alfred said: "That's for sure. And it would be easier to find someone to mow if the Corinius Family (from the township's 'We're-Better-Than-You-Folks' Swedish section) wouldn't have erected that tall, pointy monument. It stands out like a sore thumb and keeps falling apart. Kinda looks like a scarecrow in a bed of pansies." Bardolph added, "Well, if they need to show off, they can just fix it themselves and we'll just quit mowing around it." Marvin the Younger said, "Well, if we're in charge of keeping the cemetery in good shape, why don't we just cement the top back on?" As usual, no action was taken.

4) If they moved to heavy machines to dig the new graves, would it really wreck the ground?

This time Oscar spoke first saying, "Aw sheepers, dose tings must veigh two-ton." Adolph asked, "Who besides Holger and some 4-H boys are still able to dig by hand?" Bardolph, the secretary and unofficial historian, said, "We'll just have to go back to letting corpses winter in granaries until the ground thaws." Marvin, of the third generation, just looked at his watch and kept his mouth shut. No action was taken, and they moved on to the next matter. Alfred reported that Alvin Berg had again asked the Cemetery Board to take up the matter regarding moss.

5) Whose job is it to wash and scrape the moss off the markers? The relatives, or the pastor's wife's?

Oscar said, "Vell, yust look at who we're serfing. If the dead could wote, how'd ya tink they'd wote on it?" No one else would touch that one so Bardolph called for the next item of discussion.

6) How could they keep the Sunday School kids from "riding horse" on the cylinder tombstones?

Alfred, asserting his authority said, "Those kids nowadays don't have any respect for anything, living or dead."

Bardolph said, "It's not a lack of respect that bothers me, but if this behavior keeps up, we might have to get some of that insurance. I can just see some newcomer's kid falling off and breaking an arm. We could get sued." Oscar and Adolph nodded either in agreement or out of drowsiness. Marvin said, "Well, I can't think of a more decent place to play than at church with other little Lutherans." No more could be—and no more was—said.

So that the Board wouldn't get too fidgety, Alfred announced that the business portion of the Annual Meeting was soon coming to an end and that there were only two more matters to bring up, a usual one and a new one. The traditional question was:

7) Did anyone think the VA or the VFW could supply some new flags for the graves of those who had founded the township and fought in the Civil War?

Oscar woke up and simply said, 'Ja, dere gettin' kinda tatturd". Bardolph and Adolph were exasperated from saying so much already and they kept quiet. Marvin said he would check with his nephew, Earl from Rapids City, at the next family get-together. As unusual, some action had finally been taken.

Alfred cleared his throat, spit some *snus* and announced the new issue which he said had been brought to his attention by a number of upstanding citizens and some of them had even paid their $3.00 family dues for the year.

8) What in the world should be done about Andreas Hjermestad's widow? She'd been hanging around his grave long after the earth had settled and seemed to go up there everyday and bawl. Some of the neighbors were getting just plain embarrassed by all that visible emotion. There was even a path worn down from the gate to where Andreas was supposedly sleeping peacefully. Should they say anything to her about her outlandish behavior, or just throw down some rye grass seed and hope she'd soon be called Home too? The cemetery was starting to look like

just any old graveyard and even a playground in some places.

Oscar said that he thought the grass idea seemed like a sensible way to settle it. The twins weren't saying anything because, well, they'd said enough for one night already, and besides, Andreas' Mrs. was their third cousin on their mother's side and her folks had come from Gudbransdal too. Oscar added, "Should ve put a lock on the gate so ve can safe the grass?" Marvin said, "Now why would we do that? It seems to me that Mrs. Hjermestad is taking care of part of our mowing problem. Maybe we should ask more people to go up there every day and bawl."

With that, Alfred said, "Is there any further business or can we have lunch?" Adolph, noticing that it was now 8:15 p.m. wanted to get home before dawn. He regained his nerve and his voice. He stood up and said, "S'pose we've done enough work for this year, but next year we'll have to take up the gopher problem and decide if we should trap 'em or drown 'em."

As usual, Bardolph called for adjournment and Adolph seconded it. All voted in favor of adjournment and coffee, and the motion passed—as usual. Alfred, who had been slipping some these past years then said, "Ja, well, I suppose we better vote on it, then," and the other board members, not wanting to embarrass Alfred, voted again on this motion. Like the first vote this one, too, was unanimous.

Alfred, about to begin his 34th year as president, then declared the meeting over for another year. Bardolph, secretary for another year, said (as usual) that because not so much had changed, there was no sense in writing up the minutes. If pressed for information, he could just change the date on 1954's minutes. (This was a practice they had been following for several years now, and was also the circumstance under which Bardolph would accept the secretary's job for another term). Bardolph had written the minutes once in longhand and that should be enough. Adolph, as usual, said "Ja, that sure sounds sensible to me." The men moved to the kitchen where The Mrs. served egg coffee and icebox cookies , as usual.

Except for reading about the meeting the next week in the Township News in the local paper, and having Alfred report on the proceedings to the pastor, the Board's official work was done, and now they could get back to their real work: talking about mowing, talking about tightening the latch on the gate and talking about painting the shed and the outdoor biffy, and having Alfred's Mrs. bring a hot dish—on behalf of the Eidfjord Lutheran Cemetery Board—to the recently bereaved.

The roots of traditional Scandinavian Lutheran thinking had again been nourished and strengthened on the South Dakota prairie.

This is most certainly true.

TOP 5 LUTHERAN FUNERAL HYMNS

UNDER HIS WINGS

HOW GREAT THOU ART

CHILDREN OF THE HEAVENLY FATHER

DEN STORE HVITE FLOK

OLD RUGGED CROSS

LUTHERANS KNEW WHY THIS SONG WAS BANNED FROM CHURCH FUNERALS

Ostentatious Swedish monument at Eidfjord Cemetery

BJORNSON
ANDREW O.
WESTBY

J
JOHNSON

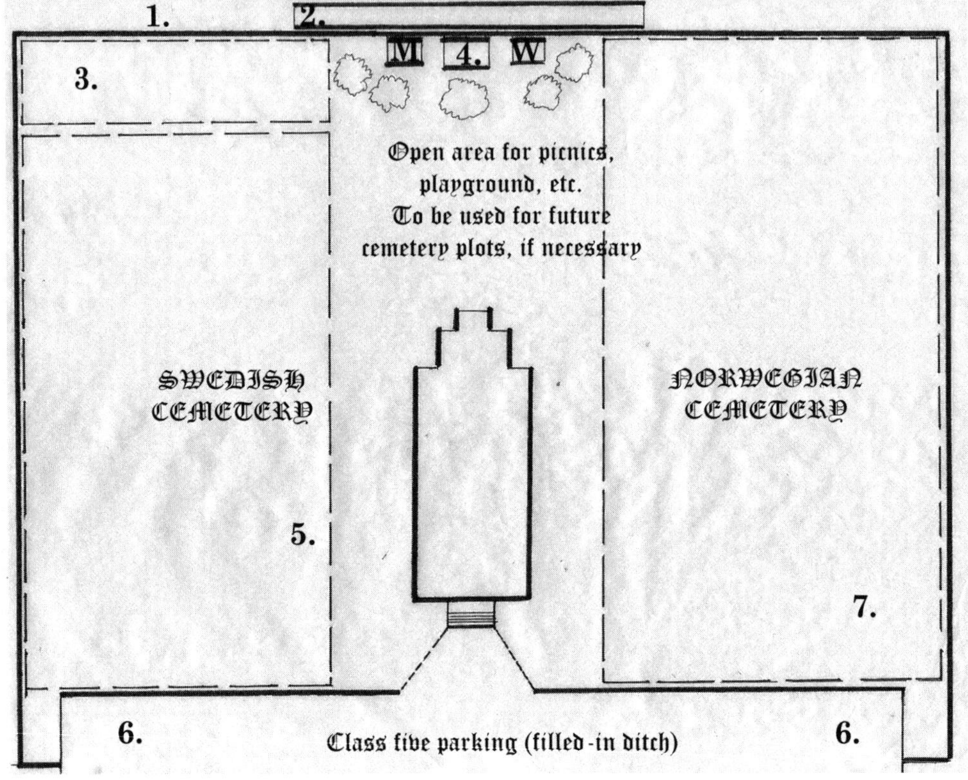

Legend:

1. Reserved for transients
2. Reserved for suicides
   (Never discussed; just known)
3. For Danes, Germans & Others
4. Tool shed
5. Ostentatious Swedish monument
6. Fence
7. Andreas Hjermestad

Part Two: How Is This Done?

Lutheran Church Basement Women

Ladies Aid - 1956

Lutheran Church Basement Women

And on the Eighth Day, God Created the Ladies Aid

God knew that if there were going to be growing, self-sustaining, active Lutheran Churches in America, he would have to create a special species of people, so He created the Lutheran Church Basement Women.

In the early Lutheran immigrant churches, services were held in homes whenever an itinerant pastor could make it. The women's group started out the same way. That is, whenever a group of women had time to get together, they would walk periodically to each other's homes—talk, do a little handiwork, exchange a few recipes, eat a little lunch and then walk home. Even though a good time was had by all, at this time in church history the women were too pooped out to elect any officers or have an agenda, and too poor to support any causes.

Then, the seeds of organization began to take root. Some of the earliest Lutheran Women's organizations were called Women's Sewing Societies or, as some men called them, Women's Gossip Societies. Women would meet, and sewing and knitting projects would be parceled out among the group. Stockings and mittens would be knit for orphans, and frivolous handiwork would be made to sell to town women. Lunches of sandwiches and beet pickles were served. Dues were ten cents, a good time was had by all, and the treasury began to grow.

By the time the men had decided to call a *prest* and build a church, the women knew that God had called them to the basement; and that's when things began to "perk." They quickly organized, elected officers (including a Historian, lest in later years, any man should boast), set up an agenda, passionately picked their causes, set dues, ate their lunch and served some egg coffee. They were *Onward Christian Soldiers* and *A Mighty Fortress* with no looking back.

As the treasury began to grow, so did the pressing needs of the congregation. The *prest* had to be paid, the parsonage had to be built, and the kitchen needed to be furnished. The Sewing Societies became The Ladies Aid and dues were raised to 15 cents. More officers were needed to help with the pressing demands of the congregation, and the women met once a month. Lunch became more elaborate, and now besides sandwiches, pickles, and cooked egg coffee, angel food cake was added to the menu. A good time was had by all, but there was much more that needed to be accomplished.

Lutheran women heeded the call and came out in droves. Because of their sizes, the Ladies Aids of a church would be split into two groups, often times referred to as East Ladies Aid and West Ladies Aid; or the South Ladies Aid Division and the North Ladies Aid Division—with each Aid congregating every other week. The faithful attended both meetings, and the treasury really began to grow. Altar pictures were purchased, pews replaced chairs, walls were repainted, the *prest* got a raise by making it known he couldn't exist on two dead chickens and eggs, stoves were upgraded, and glorified rice and a bigger variety of sandwiches and cakes were added to the menu, but, because of the Depression, the dues remained the same. The meetings got longer, the coffee got better (thanks to the new stove) and a good time was still had by all.

But, like the fish and loaves story in the Bible, a real miracle was needed. The congregation had outgrown its sanctuary, Sunday School was splitting at the seams, and the mission field was calling. And with God's help, the ladies of the Aid, the backbone of the church and the keepers of the purse strings, came up with the fish and the loaves. They began to meet weekly. To raise money, they organized dinners—harvest, *lutefisk*, kraut and sausage. They served a noon meal dinner (open to the men) adding hotdish, Jell-O and buttered bread to the menu—as well as ten more cents to the price. Through their efforts, bigger churches were built and others were remodeled. Homemade wooden tables and chairs in the basement were replaced with new stackable tables with kick-down metal legs and new metal chairs. Tract Racks were installed, Sunday School material was bought and furnaces were replaced. They served weddings, funerals and other doings "to pay back Peter and to pay back Paul." Nobody dared to question the worth of the Ladies Aid. However, at this time, a good time was not had by all.

Even though all Lutheran women felt a sense of obligation to heathen women in parts of the world like Africa, China, and Alaska, how to best help became the issue. Some thought it should be done within the confines of the local Ladies Aid, and others wanted to become part of a larger group known as the Lutheran Women's Missionary Federation. Eventually, over coffee and bars, it all became ironed out and the Women's Missionary Federation became a powerful national force in the Lutheran church. Organizations such as Dorcas Society and Young's Women's Missionary Society were outgrowths of this organization. Hospitals, orphanages, and homes for the unwed were supported with both financial and emotional support. As Widow Snustad said, "I love adoption, it's such a modest way to have a baby." Once again, the women came through, and a good time was had by all.

The ladies continued to carry the torch, taking on more responsibilities on the home fronts as well as in the foreign fields. They organized into Circles, with names such as The Ruth Circle, The Esther Circle, The Morning Circle, The Young Mother's Circle, The Evening Circle, and The Praying Paying Phoebes Circle. They poked their heads out of the basement long enough to pay for and furnish educational wings, youth rooms, fireside rooms, nurseries, bride's rooms, elevators, and wallpaper for the first floor bathrooms. They continued to serve wherever and whenever they were called. They might have changed their name, and they might have changed their menus, but God knew what He was doing when on the eighth day He created The Lutheran Church Basement Women.

This is most certainly true.

And the Women Created Committees

Once the ladies became more organized than the army, it didn't take them long to create more committees and protocol than the Pentagon.

The Nominating Committee:

The nominating committee was in charge of selecting the upcoming officers. As Widow Snustad said each year to the committee, "They must be of the highest moral caliber. It is really a call from both God and your neighbor ladies."

The President:

The president of the Ladies Aid had the highest calling in the church basement. She not only had to call the meeting to order and know what was going on, but she also had to always look presentable, i.e., seams straight, foundation garment in place, and be attired in proper hat and gloves if the members were to have confidence in her ability to pull things together.

The Vice President:

The vice—president, second in command, had to be prepared to take over if the President took ill. She had a tough position, because like a Confirmand at Catechization, she never knew when she would be called on to answer.

The Secretary:

The secretary had to pay attention and not daydream or any errors in her "minutes of the last meeting" which she read at the next meeting could and would be called into question.

The Historian:

This woman had to know how to write legibly in both English and the mother tongue of the congregation whether it be Norwegian, German, Swedish or Danish. She had to record the doings without showing bias. (Widow Snustad was never elected to this position).

The Treasurer:

The treasurer had to be honest and above reproach. She kept the money in a box at her home, and her records always had to be open to anyone (including Widow Snustad) who had questions.

The Mission Committee:

This committee was in charge of getting the supplies ready to send to the foreign mission fields. They also lined up local mission projects like bringing baskets to the shut-ins, etc.

The Lunch Committee:

This committee had to decide what would be a standard fare to serve at funerals, harvest festivals, *lutefisk* suppers, mission festivals, weddings, ladies aid, auctions, and whether they should serve anything between services.

The Food Kitchen Committee:

This committee had to decide when to use a Ladies Aid cut, an angel food cut, a funeral cut, or a regular cut when cutting a cake. They decided when a doings called for a plain red Jell-0 or when a large banana should be sliced into it. They had to "post" how many eggs, how many scoops of coffee and how many quarts of water it took to make a church basement sized white enameled pot full of egg coffee. They were the ones who let the funeral committee know how many red Jell-O's, how much "dead spread," how many cakes and how many jars of pickles it took to serve 154 mourners.

The Kitchen Proper Committee:

This committee made sure the insurance companies had donated enough napkins, checked to make sure utensils and silverware were in adequate supply and dishes weren't chipped. They made sure the stove was always in working order. They submitted the list of "recommendation of things needed for the kitchen" which was voted on at the general meetings.

The Serving Committee:

This committee served the food at the church functions, and made sure that the food was always served in an orderly and proper fashion. They knew how to get people through the food lines without a whole lot of commotion. They knew which tablecloths were used for which functions. They knew how to get the kitchen counter doors up and down without creating a lot of noise. They also knew where on the linoleum the tables should be placed to create the most space.

The Clean-Up Committee:

This committee washed the dishes, put them back in their proper spots, wiped off the counters and tables, took down the tables, put away the tablecloths, and took home the dishtowels for laundering.

These were but a few of the committees it took to operate a smooth running Ladies Aid.

This is most certainly true.

Bars & Jell-O

An Inside Glimpse of a Lutheran Church Basement Kitchen

Hours and hours of Ladies Aid time was taken up with kitchen issues. Although there were no fist fights among the Ladies Aid women, kitchen issues at Aid meetings became as "hot" an issue as the kitchen itself did during a *lutefisk* supper. Some of the issues were:

• If the kitchen is going to have to double as a Sunday School room on Sunday mornings, should we put a lock on the sugar lump cupboard?

• If a member of the church is not in good standing, should they be allowed to used the lace tablecloths for a wedding reception in the church parlor? If so, who cleans them?

• What do you say to a kitchen worker who drops a cup, then just says "*Uffda*, but I'm clumsy" and doesn't offer to put a little extra in the Aid offering to cover the cost?

• If a Lutheran lady is known to have gray-tinged wash hanging on her lines every Monday morning, and she offers to take home the dishtowels to wash, how do you handle this issue in a Christian way?

When the kitchen was going to undergo a complete remodeling, things really heated up. All ladies (except the pastor's wife) and a few town women had worked in the kitchen, and all were experts. They all knew what was the best kind of stove to buy, where the salt and pepper shakers should go, which pattern of dishes would look the best with the other decor in the basement, what color the counter linoleum should be, and on and on and on. Some, like Widow Snustad who did as little as possible in the kitchen, thought Aid money should go to the missions instead of a new kitchen. Others, who basically lived in the kitchen, argued that with a bigger kitchen more people could be served—thus the treasury would grow, ensuring even more money for the missions. It was always a no win situation, but the needs of the kitchen were usually a priority.

Standard ingredients for a well-equipped Lutheran Church Basement Kitchen should include:

*sturdy cupboards that most could reach
*a cupboard wide enough to store salt and pepper shakers for all the tables
*a cupboard wide enough to store sugar bowls for all the tables
*a cupboard for pressed glass pickle dishes
*a cupboard for pressed glass serving trays that were used for buns and cakes
*several cupboards or shelves for water glasses
*several cupboards for coffee cups
*several cupboards for plates
*several cupboards for butter plates
*several cupboards for kettles large enough to boil potatoes and *lutefisk*
*several cupboards for enameled coffee pots
*several cupboards for nectar pitchers
*drawers deep enough to store several potato mashers
*drawers deep enough to store LB and AAL napkins
*drawers deep enough to store dishtowels, dishrags, and potholders
*several drawers to store silverware and serving pieces
*several drawers to store miscellaneous items such as potato peelers
*linoleum counters that would blend in and be easy to clean
*a stove that had all burners working and was easy to light
*a refrigerator large enough to put funeral flowers in (if a family left them to be used for the church altar the Sunday after the funeral), and to store Jell-0's, eggs, and a pint jar of cream, but not so big and wasteful that a freezer compartment would be included. (This was a frivolous option, because ice cubes

were never needed in a Lutheran Church Basement)

*a place for the garbage cans
*a place for the slop pail
*a place for mops and buckets
*a place for miscellaneous rags
*a place for soap
*a place to set wet dishtowels
*a center working table which could be used as a Sunday School table, if needed
*a special drawer for funeral tablecloths
*a special place for wedding tablecloths
*a special place for everyday tablecloths
*a place to hang aprons
*a place to put purses
*two stools for buttering buns.

This is most certainly true.

Rolling bandages for the leper colonies

Lutheran Church Basement Women's Aprons: The Basic Six

1. *The Serving Apron:*

This was the 'Lutheran Standard' of all aprons. Most Lutheran women who were willing workers and willing servers owned several of these 24 inch long, slightly pressed, gathered and tied at the waist, flowered or gingham-checked, cotton serving aprons. Adorned with only one handy pocket, these aprons were not used for heavy duty serving.

2. *The Anniversary Apron:*

This apron was worn by Lutheran women who served silver and golden wedding anniversaries in the church basement. Most people who weren't Lutheran couldn't tell the difference between this apron and a serving apron. Lutheran women could. The gingham-checked aprons usually had some cross-stitch running across the bottom of the apron, and the flowered one had a couple of rows of rickrack or trim on them to dress them up a little bit.

3. *The Wedding Apron:*

Lutheran brides purchased these little, white, lacy and see-through (not risqué though), stiff, organza aprons for friends and family members who served at their wedding. Given as a gift to the waitresses, they were usually put in a closet and never used again. They were impractical and a waste of good money, but they were necessary and appropriate attire for coffee servers at Lutheran weddings.

4. *The Catch-All Apron:*

Because they covered Lutheran servers from the shoulders to the knees, this all-purpose, understated apron was a favorite for Lutheran women when they were heavy duty serving. Some Lutheran men wore them when they were cooking for mother-daughter banquets. Loaded with pockets, they were practical but not pretty. In Lutheran homes these aprons were usually hung up and not folded in drawers.

5. *The Everday Apron:**

These were the worn out serving and catch-all aprons that Lutheran women wore around their homes and only wore in church when they were doing the annual spring and fall cleaning of the church basement.

6. *The Dishtowel Apron:*

This was another apron worn by both Lutheran women and Lutheran men. Lutheran women wore them in a pinch when for some reason or another they forgot their appropriate apron at home; but Lutheran men who did dishes at mother-daughter banquets used them without thinking a thing about it. Some Lutherans threw them over their shoulder when cooking so they had something to wipe their hands on, or they used them as potholders when the unexpected came up.

This is most certainly true.

**Fancy people pronounced it "every day".*

This is taken from Lutheran Church Basement Women by Janet Letnes Martin and Allen Todnem. Redbird Productions, 1992.

Types of Lutheran Church Basement Women

Mary Types—The Listeners	Martha Types—The Doers
Gives devotions	Organizes kitchen crew
Serves coffee	Makes coffee
Arranges centerpieces	Sets and cleans tables
Wears high heel shoes and nylons	Wears wedgies and anklets
Wears fancy aprons	Wears everyday aprons
Introduces speakers	Serves speakers
Plays piano	Dusts piano
Visits with speaker	Washes dishes
Arranges for next speaker	Takes down tables and cleans up
Announces meeting	Serves next meeting

This is taken from Lutheran Church Basement Women by Janet Letnes Martin and Allen Todnem. Redbird Productions, 1992.

Twenty Statements that Lutheran Women Can't Say, but Might Think!

1. That's the fourth time she has used that excuse.
2. They're dying likes flies around here. If I have to bring another cake, I think I'll scream.
3. Don't call me for anything. I'm too busy.
4. Get some of the younger ones to do it.
5. If we run out, that's just too bad.
6. I don't want to listen to your complaints. I've got enough troubles.
7. Tell her to cater it!
8. It's about time we started using paper cups.
9. She hasn't been in church for ages, then shows up for the banquet. Figures!
10. I don't know how she dares to ask us to serve.
11. We're not a restaurant for crying out loud.
12. I can't work. (No explanation given.)
13. Who does she think she is anyway?
14. What do we have a janitor for anyway?
15. I haven't seen the pastor's wife get her hands in a sink of water.
16. Nobody needs a big meal for a 3 o'clock funeral, that's for sure.
17. Life's not a bowl of cherries for anyone.
18. She isn't the only one who has got other commitments.
19. Let's keep it simple.
20. Why do Lutherans think they have to eat every time they go to church?

This is taken from Lutheran Church Basement Women by Janet Letnes Martin and Allen Todnem. Redbird Productions, 1992.

Twenty Statements Heard by Proper, Cheerful, Lutheran Basement Women

1. It's nothing.
2. I'm sorry.
3. You sit down and let me do it.
4. I will be more than happy to help.
5. What can I bring then?
6. Don't think a thing about it.
7. I'll stand. I've been sitting all morning.
8. *Mange tusen takk.*
9. Give me the dishtowel. It's my turn now.
10. You've had a long day. Sit down then.
11. I haven't had my turn.
12. I have nothing better to do.
13. I can easily double the recipe.
14. It's *ingenting.*
15. Keep the dishes coming.
16. Give me the dishtowels. I'm washing tomorrow anyway.
17. I'm not helpless.
18. I can be there by 6 in the morning.
19. It's about time I return the favor.
20. Keep me posted. I can get there in a flash.

This is taken from Lutheran Church Basement Women by Janet Letnes Martin and Allen Todnem. Redbird Productions, 1992.

A place to put purses

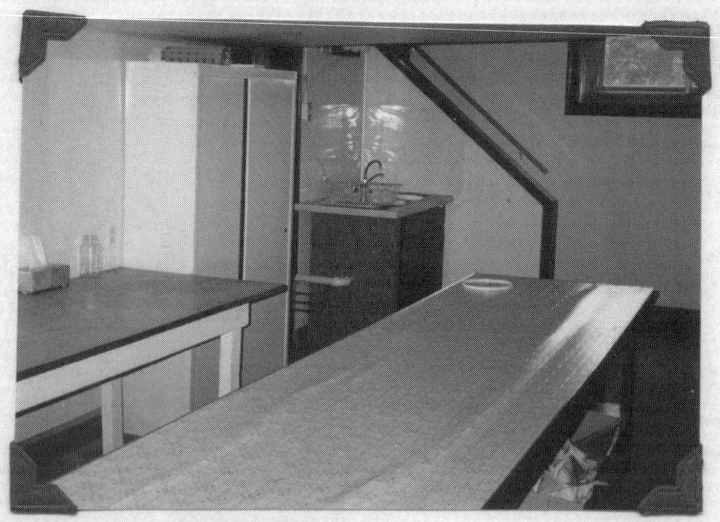

An easy-to-clean linoleum counter

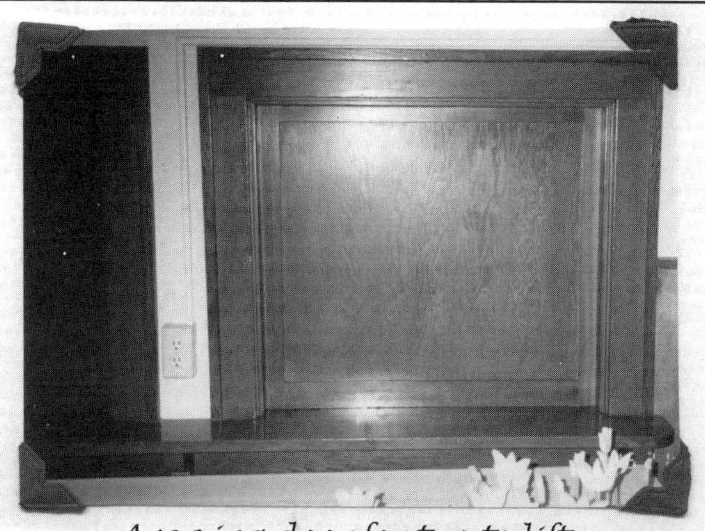

A serving door for two to lift

Orderly, categorized, everything-in-its-place Lutheran drawers and cupboards

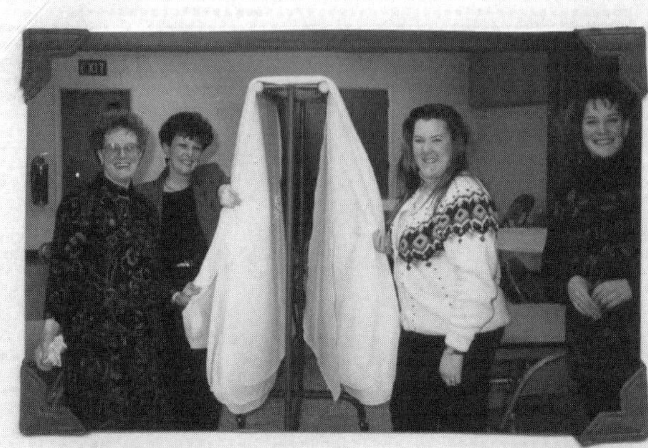

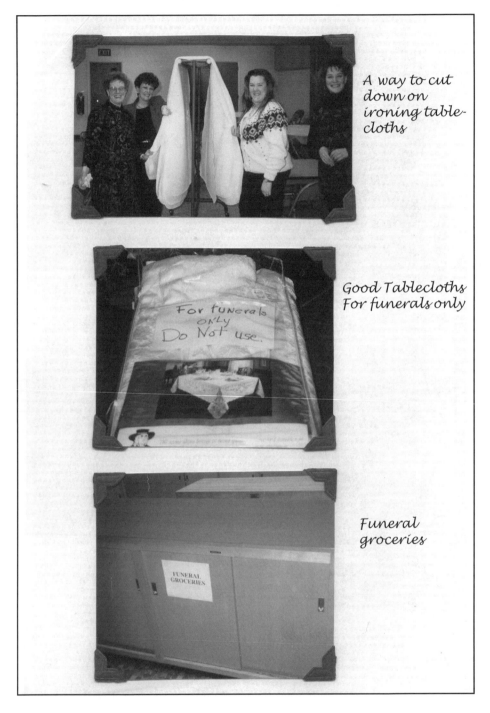

A way to cut down on ironing table-cloths

Good Tablecloths For funerals only

Funeral groceries

Fair are the Meadows: The Summer the Aid met up with the World

The women of Trefoldighet Lutheran had never had to beg for money before 1957 when the Luther Leaguers started to think that they would be better Christian kids if they could travel away from home to attend conventions. Up until 57 the women had generated enough money from church supper "per plate" charges to keep the kitchen stocked with good tablecloths and enough kettles to handle just about any doings. They had also helped purchase the new electric Hammond organ so the congregation could get rid of that big overbearing pipe organ that had just stood there collecting dust since the 20's. They had generated enough money to provide baptismal certificates for all the babies. Of course, that number had dropped considerably since the war, and now they were spending more time spreading funeral buns than signing baptismal certificates. But, they had done these things and done them without hawking and begging or resorting to other unchristian tasks like the Methodists and Catholics had done. On top of all this, they had given their annual benevolence to the foreign missions, and had zealously brought cheer and hotdishes to the poorly via the Sunshine Club. Sometimes it seemed like their motto should be: "If it ain't one thing, it's another." Anyway, this sure seemed to sum up how they operated and then besides, no one could argue with common sense like that.

But now, in the era of Orville Freeman and Coya Knutson and Ike, the Luther Leaguers had decided that they, too, could do more good out in the world. Thus it was that the Trefoldighet Ladies Aid swallowed their pride and donned their wedgies and headed for the county fair where they would have a food booth like those other religions. As Aid President Tekla Swanson said, "If God wants our children to go ye out and spread the Gospel in '58, He must *also* be telling us to go forth. I guess our mission field is right here in the county seat for four days each summer. We better start serving, and we better start now. If the prices keep going up, there's no telling where they'll stop and it would be a shame if the League didn't have enough money to send some delegates to the convention in Missoula." Well, the ladies couldn't argue with that and even if they would have wanted to, they wouldn't have done so because they were Scandinavian Lutheran. Thus it was that the women of Trefoldighet rented a food stand at the Fillmore, MN County Fair in 1957.

The stand had been operated by Calvary Baptist through 1956 when the Baptists said, "Of all people, *we have* to have water and we're getting to old to haul it. If the fair board doesn't put in running water, we'll just have to quit," and so they did. Of course, being Baptist, they had higher uses for water than most religions did and had left the booth in a mess. The first job for the Trefoldighet Aid was to clean the booth and they voted to put Pearl Peterson in charge of the cleanup crew. The vote was unanimous as their votes always were. No one in Trefoldighet Ladies Aid wanted to make a scene or stand out so they all went along with whatever was said first. This seemed more Christian than arguing and besides, the meetings went faster so they had more time to chat and catch up on the news. Pearl, knowing that people are called in different ways, accepted the job as she always did. She and Emma Jensen were appointed to scout out the facility and report back to the group at the next meeting.

At the March meeting, Pearl and Emma gave their report. Pearl had driven Emma to Preston where she was doctoring and so they had decided to make a day of it. After Emma's appointment, the two of them spent some time visiting old friends in The Home, and then they had gone to the fairgrounds. They knew it would be muddy so they had left their Kickerinos at home and taken their everday overshoes. They parked along side the road and crawled through the fence hoping that Roy, the big-town constable, wouldn't see them. Actually, they hoped that no one at all would see them. Well, they had some mighty interesting information to report back to the group.

This fair booth stuff was going to be a mighty challenging endeavor for the families of Trefoldighet. Some of the women would have to take their children along when they worked their shifts, and the kids would be exposed to town people and carnies and all kinds of riffraff. Furthermore, the women who didn't drive (which was all of them except Pearl and the new Mrs. John Olson, nee Doris Carlson), would have to have their husbands bring them to the fair and when the men were waiting for the women's shifts to get over, they would, of course, have to look around at the machinery and at the booths under the grandstand and chances were pretty good that their men would see some of those slinky carnival women with the short-shorts on, and the men could be exposed to all sorts of temptations. And now for the real challenge. The new food booth was located next to the booth run by the "KC's"—the Knights of Columbus from St. Stanislov's in the county seat. The Ladies Aid women would be there in the midst of town people and carnies and Bohemians and along side of Catholics all at the same time. The women of Trefoldighet's Ladies Aid began to more fully grasp the meaning of the phrase, "The Lord works in mysterious ways." What was He calling them to do?

Well, sure as shootin', the booth got cleaned and the groceries were bought and the assignments were made and the fair began. Right from the get-go, the women found the whole experience exciting, although they never admitted it. They also found it theologically taxing to work where they were next door to Catholic men, could hear the Midway barkers, and where every once in a while, some carnival woman whose earrings were bigger than her pants, would walk by. As Anna Skog said, "*Nei, fy da.*"

Like all Lutheran women, the women in the booth sweat a lot, but it was a different kind of sweat than that in the church basement. This was more of a mental sweat. It poured down their foreheads instead of their arms, and gave many women headaches. By the last day, no one wanted the job even though it was a good moneymaker for the youth. Agnes Gjermundson, who was having one of her spells, said that she would volunteer to clean the church all by herself for Easter if she didn't have to pull that sinful fair duty anymore.

Because the Trefoldighet Lunch Stand was closer to the Midway than to the 4-H barns, the whole experience seemed even less Christian. Evelyn Tingvold said that from their booth she had seen one of the Ness boys throw a ring over a pop bottle for a some foam-rubber dice. Coaxed on by the carnies, one of their own flock was now gambling right out in the open, and this was the same Ness boy that she had lent money to in church for the birthday bank last November! Mavis Tunheim reported that she had seen the Prestvold kid shoot a BB gun at some plastic ducks trying to get them to flip over in the water at the very same time that his dad was slaving away on the tractor at The Homeplace trying to get the wet hay to flip over and dry. Olga Lestevold said she found it just plain awful that some men customers from town sat at their Lutheran booth and talked about the two-headed lady just like she was a freak calf or something.

It seemed that each shift had a horror story to report. Mildred Holmquist said that she was afraid she might see one of Trefoldighet's youth smoking cigarettes near the barns. Well, of course, this concern spread like wildfire from shift to shift, but it really was nothing to get all hot and bothered about because the Lutheran kids who met town kids at the fair were too smart to smoke by the barns where the older Lutherans would linger. The Lutheran kids who tried smoking met their town acquaintances behind the Fisheries Building that was full of northerns and walleyes and turtles because they knew the women of the church didn't like reptiles and would never go near that building even though the exhibits were free.

The Trefoldighet kids who were at the fair were warned hourly by the women of the church to stay away from the carnies so they wouldn't get kidnapped. Like Mrs. Halvor T. Halvorson said about the carnies, "Those people certainly aren't Scandinavian or Lutheran. Where in the world do they come from, and how in the world do they get that way?" This lead the women of Trefoldighet Ladies Aid to begin having some serious discussions. Should they spend their time trying to evangelize to the carnies for some eternal good, or keep making material money at the booth for the youth and other mission fields? Was there really a mission field right here at the fair grounds and if so, or were they, the Lutheran women, treading on territory rightly belonging to the Mormons and Jehovah's Witnesses? They began these discussions, but never took them far. Dishing up raisin pie and Blond Betty bars was a lot easier than having deep thoughts.

While some of the women were concerned about the spiritual life of the carnies, the new Mrs. John Olson (nee Doris Carlson), was more concerned about their social conditions. Before she became Mrs. Olson, she had kind of thought about being a county extension agent, and she secretly wondered if her training in 4-H and Homemakers Club couldn't be put to use with these gypsies. The carny men wore sandals and white rayon shirts unbuttoned halfway down their chests; nothing substantial. The carny women hardly wore anything at all—except maybe a midriff or something. Doris thought maybe the Trefoldighet 4-H girls who had taken blue or purple on the outfits they entered at the fair could teach the carny women how to sew. Doris knew the carnies all lived in trailer houses on wheels, and wondered what kind of life that was for a family with their kids eating cotton candy and snow cones all day long, and spinning on the Tilt-a-Whirl whenever they wanted to. Doris thought maybe there was something the 4-H boys could do too, like teach the carny men and boys some construction, or maybe the 4-H'rs could just teach them about nutrition or hygiene or something like that. Doris realized that these thoughts were a wee bit too liberal for the Trefoldighet women so she—like Mary—kept all these things and pondered them in her heart, and got back to serving pie.

At the Trefoldighet Booth a roast beef dinner cost a buck. With it one got mashed potatoes, gravy, sliced beef, corn, cloverleaf buns, coleslaw, beet pickles (which turned the bordering foods maroon), lemonade and coffee. Pie was extra.

This was the one church event for which the women didn't have to make homemade bread. They just bought buns at the store. They served dinner from 11:00 a.m. to 1:00 p.m. At 1:00, the women cleaned up the lunch stand and from 2:00 to 4:00 p.m., they served coffee and apple, lemon or raisin pie for 25 cents.

After dinner, the women who pulled the afternoon shift took turns cleaning up the booth (with water they hauled over from the barns) so that half of them could go to the 4-H Building to see what canning and what garments "took blue". Then they went to check the barns to see what their kids got on their animals, and they used that time to again remind the Trefoldighet youngsters to behave, and to stay away from the Midway, and from town kids who had cigarettes in their rolled-up sleeves. The moms hoped their kids would remember what they had already been taught, and that the kids would realize that the Midway scene really had nothing at all to do with their Lutheran heritage—even if the Ladies Aid had a booth at the fair.

From 4:30 to 6:30 p.m. the Ladies Aid served a roast beef supper with the same trappings. Then the women cleaned up again and cleared out of there before the loud music started blaring and the stock car races started, and before the fairgrounds started to look like Sin City and the real trash came out.

In the morning it started all over again. The women arrived and parked in the ditches along the main road, except for the one lady had a pass to drive in and deliver groceries to the booth. By the time they got set up again, the KC's—who had been up half the night playing Bingo on the Midway—had already been serving for an hour.

In the morning the KC's served up pancakes and sausage; at noon they served spaghetti and meatballs; and by early afternoon they were dispensing brats and beer. It was pretty easy for the Lutherans to spot the Catholics because most of their men had tomatoey stuff running down the fronts of their Dacron shirts, and their women had a whole tribe of kids trailing them and were headed straight for the Midway. Other than the money the women could make for the Youth Convention, the one good thing about the fair was that because the Catholics were easy to spot, the Lutheran kids knew who to stay away from.

Then too, the booth at the Fillmore County Fair had been kind of a good experience for the women of Trefoldighet because it had forced them to think about some things they would rather not have had to think about. But most of all, this fair fundraiser was a sobering reminder to the congregation that if everyone gave their ten percent, there would be no need for this worldly fair booth business. The women of Trefoldighet made that perfectly clear to the congregation when they all got back together in September for Rally Day. They also made sure that all the kids knew what sacrifices the women of Trefoldighet had made for their youth, and that they—the women of Trefoldighet—would take no sass for a long time and the kids didn't have to assume that the Ladies Aid women would be making barbecues and hot cocoa for every League meeting, and the convention delegates better be prepared to give a full report to the congregation at a Temple Talk in the Fall!

To be sure, the whole fair experience had left its mark on everyone in the Trefoldighet Congregation, but once the women knew that everyone else knew what they had gone through, the women of Trefoldighet began making plans for the next year's fair booth, and kind of looked forward to watching those KC's from St. Stanislov's live it up a little again.

This is most certainly true.

Feeding the 5000 Over and Over Again

Feasts, Festival and High Holy Days

Just paging through the liberal green hymnal, one comes across terms such as festivals, major feast days and minor feast days as well as lists of unheard of people with unpronounceable names who now have a special day set aside in their honor. During the black and early red hymnal eras there were festivals and there were feast days and they basically had to do with menus, fundraising, and a lot of hard work.

There were two major festivals: the Fall Harvest Festival and the Mission Supper, and one minor festival, John Deere Day. There were two yearly major feast days: the *Lutefisk* Supper and the annual Sunday School Picnic; one major monthly feast day, the Ladies Aid Dinner; and three minor feast days; the Mother-Daughter Banquet, the Father-Son Banquet, and the Pancake Breakfast put on by the youth as a fundraiser so they could send delegates to the national Luther League Convention.

In addition, there were two events that were too close to call; a farm auction lunch of barbecues, bars and coffee served by the Ladies Aid for a longtime member of the church who was in good standing but who, for one reason or another (who's to judge then), had a run of tough luck, and an ice cream social on the church grounds. In addition, the lunch stand at the county fair (See chapter on the Ladies Aid) might be a week to partake of good Lutheran cooking, but because of all the shady people in attendance, this event couldn't—in good Christian conscience—be considered part of the church calendar.

Lutefisk Suppers: The Scandinavian Lutheran Version of Fishes and Loaves

If Scandinavian Lutherans could add one more feast day to the church calendar, it would be the feast of fish and flatbread or, as it would be called in Norwegian, *En festlig middag av fisk og flatbrød.* Unlike the Catholics who had to eat fish every Friday, Scandinavian Lutherans were only morally obligated to eat it once a year, and that was at the annual *Lutefisk* Supper.

As Tellef Klemetson once said to a stubborn German Lutheran who farmed the 80 next to his, "Of course it's Biblical! Jesus fed the 5000 with fish and bread, and since they all went away full and satisfied, it had to have been *lutefisk* and *flatbrød.* Just look it up!" But the stubborn German knew it was really a fundraiser in disguise, but then money changers in the temple was Biblical too! Scandinavian Lutherans, however, believed differently, and even unto this day have their theological differences with the German Lutherans.

And it came to pass that the annual Church Basement *Lutefisk* Supper was kind of a holy day for Scandinavian Lutherans. It was a day of great anticipation and much preparedness, whether you came to eat or came to serve. It was a day when everyone in the church cleaned up, showed up, and sat together to partake in a meal of Scandinavian Holy Food.

The supper and all of its trimmings, trappings, committee assignments, and preparations didn't vary much from Lutheran church to Lutheran church. The meal usually began somewhere between 4:00 and 4:30 p.m. and was served until 8:30 to accommodate those who milked. However, by 3:30 some of the faithful who didn't have much to do because they had retired and moved to town and couldn't wait any longer, had showed up and taken their places upstairs in the pews to await the calling of the ticket numbers. The ones who arrived at 3:30 had time to sit, think, reflect and worry about whether the roads would turn bad before they got out of there, and whether or not the fish would be as good this year as it was last year.

As people poured into the pews, the pianist began to play hymns for people to sing as they waited for "the call." When the pianist, Gerda Martinson, was in the middle of *When the Roll is Called Up Yonder* or another good old golden oldie, Mrs. Einar Stensrud would periodically climb the steps up to the sanctuary in her comfortable brown oxfords and loudly announce, "*Vær så god*. Tickets 69-99 may now come downstairs."

Everything was done in an orderly hushed fashion. There was no pushing or shoving. There were no food fights. Everything about it seemed white and pure. The tables were covered and draped in white tablecloths. White snow that clung to Lutheran overshoes was stomped off unto the linoleum floor. White dishtowels were slung over the shoulders of the sweaty kitchen workers.

Large, no-nonsense, blonde Lutheran ladies mashed kettle after kettle of white potatoes and white rutabagas without complaining. Smaller and older white-haired Lutheran ladies with noticeable dowager's humps sat on stools in the kitchen arranging plates of off-white *lefse* and white Scandinavian goodies such as *krumkaker, berlinerkranser, fattigmann,* rosettes, spritz, and white sugar cookies. Those who were a little straighter but not strong enough to mash, stirred the creamy white *rømmegrøt* and poured it into small sauce dishes.

The translucent, white, jellylike *lutefisk*, encased in white cheese cloth, was carefully lifted out of the boiling water. It looked like white-gauzed Sunday School angels. Immediately it was heaped unto white platters and was brought to the tables along with the rest of the food.

As the fish was carefully and reverently passed down the banquet table from one Scandinavian to another, all idle chatter ceased. Only words such as "*mange takk*" and "*takk*" could be heard. The room became as quiet as it did when the Sunday School superintendent started the singing of *The Lord is in His Holy Temple* at the beginning of opening exercises.

As Ole Langerud poured the melted butter over the fish on his plate, he stared at the fish as if in a trance, shuddered, and thought to himself, "this almost looks sanctified, then."

As the plate of flatbrød was passed, the person at the table who was nearest to the center church basement pole, broke off a section of the dry, unleavened bread and without even looking up, passed it on to the Scandinavian farmer who sat south of him. As Ole Langerud was breaking off a good-sized piece of *flatbrød*, he again shuddered and thought to himself, "Well, this is kind of like communion, then."

The meal was always eaten in good will and harmony. There wasn't a seating arrangement. There wasn't a head table, and there wasn't even a smattering of Lutheran high church protocol. In other words, there were no reserved pews. These diners were—in the words of Martin Luther—one in thought, word, and deed. The church president might be sitting by the shy, Norwegian bachelor farmer, Per Glomsrud, who had cleaned up and come into town to eat *lutefisk*. Miss Fititude, Fern Mortensen, might have to sit by the disheveled Swensson's and their big brood of kids. But at the *Lutefisk* Supper, nothing but the fish mattered to Scandinavian Lutherans. They knew that if you took a slab of dried cod, soaked it in water and then in poison, and finally cleansed it in water, it became just like the fishes and loaves story in the Bible—truly a miracle.

This is most certainly true.

Note: If you have never been to a supper or are curious about how to prepare food for 5000 Scandinavians who read for the minister, just take 4.16 times this recipe for 1200 and you should be fine. If you want to know why these hard-working, seemingly normal people eat this food, ask any good Norwegian Lutheran pastor with Haugean leanings who likes to argue.

Lutefisk Dinner for 1200

600 pounds of *lutefisk*
400 pounds of meatballs
116 pounds of butter
600 pounds of potatoes
276 cans of corn
40 gallons of cold slaw
40 quarts of dill pickles
20 quarts of beet pickles
600 pieces of *flatbrød*
2000 pieces of *lefse*
20 loaves of rye bread (for the Swedes)
60 dozen buns
3500 cups of coffee
Between 5000-6000 Scandinavian cookies such as *krumkake*, spritz, etc.

*Vær så god!**

Recipe taken from Second Helpings of Cream and Bread by Janet Letnes Martin and Allen Todnem. Redbird Productions, 1986.

The Harvest Festival: 1 and 2

Harvest Festival #1

Most Lutheran churches held a Fall Supper, sometimes called the Harvest Festival. Even though there was mention of a Harvest Festival in the book of Exodus, it became, as Gertrude Stensrud disgustingly told Millie Hendahl, "just another thinly disguised fundraiser. If people just gave their ten percent, we wouldn't have to resort to these heathen tactics."

Sometime in late October—before the *Lutefisk* Supper and before boy's basketball was in full swing taking on the neighboring rivals, but after the harvest moon, and when the corn and potatoes were all up—the basement windows in Lutheran churches across the country were all steamed up from pans of chicken frying, roasters full of ham baking and meatballs browning, potatoes boiling and garden vegetables simmering . Apple pies made from a good crop of windfalls were bubbling over in the ovens as people were filing into the basement.

Members and even people from other faiths in town came to partake of this freewill offering meal and join in what was billed as "good clean family fun and fellowship." Men came to eat and to take home the women who worked in the kitchen but didn't drive. Women in wedgies unabashedly came and walked in a circle on a circle of numbers that had been chalked on the floor hoping to win a nice, high, angelfood cake on the cakewalk. Kids came to stand in front of a blanket thrown over a Sunday School divider to "fish" for a bottle of bubbles, bookmark, candy or another appropriate Lutheran trinket from the fish pond.

It was like an open house in the basement of the church from 5:00 to 8:00 in the evening not to "gather together to thank Thee, our Maker," as Gertrude Stensrud wrote in her anonymous letter to the pastor and church council, but to gather together to make up for the dip in summer giving. Even though Lutheran women brazenly hawked their wares of crocheted potholders, Sunday-Monday-Tuesday dishtowels, and cross-stitched gingham aprons that had been placed in and amongst the pumpkin, gourd and Indian-corn center-pieced tables, they knew in their hearts that: 1) since the meal was a freewill offering, they might be feeding the needy, and 2) they would never get carried away and bring bingo to the basement like some churches down the road apiece did.

This is most certainly true.

Harvest Festival #2

Some members of conservative Lutheran churches who had made sure that their constitution forbade any basement selling still pulled off a harvest festival and took in some much needed cash. They used the theme "Harvest of Blessing," served ham and all the trimmings, and had the pastor challenge those who had been blessed with a good crop to give until it hurt. Usually this piling on of Lutheran guilt worked, but then again, some just ate their ham, put in their dollar, and went home.

This is most certainly true.

Mission Festival: When Minnesotans Met the Malagasies

After the Ladies Aid joined up with the Women's Missionary Federation, interest in supporting foreign mission fields was a top priority. When the missionaries came home on furlough, they didn't have time for rest and relaxation, because they spent their time showing slides and giving programs to Lutheran congregations at what became known as The Mission Festival. The Mission Festival was billed as a family night for the whole congregation.

Most Lutheran children growing up in the Lutheran church were taught about missionaries and the foreign mission field when they were in Sunday School. Lutheran children could point out on a map where countries such as Formosa, North Borneo, Tanganyika, Zululand, Malagasy, and Madagascar (where Utemba lived) were located.

At home, when Lutheran children turned up their noses at things like *lutefisk* or liver, they were once again given a mission lesson by their mothers who would say, "Just be thankful you have something to eat. Think about all the starving children in Madagascar who would be thankful for such food." (Kids usually knew better.) However, when the missionaries came to a Lutheran church to share their slides and stories, there was usually something on the potluck supper table that kids would eat without complaining.

The Mission Festival was usually held on a Saturday or Sunday. It was usually held in the church basement with food and a slide show, followed by a question and answer period. Three hymns that the congregation usually sang at this festival were *Lost in the Night Do the Heathens Yet Languish, From Greenland's Icy Mountains,* and *I Love to Tell the Story.*

The kids loved the slide show. It was the closest thing to a movie that some Lutheran children had ever seen. They had seen pictures of heathens in the National Geographic, and wondered if the missionary would dare show any slides of heathens that were just too naked to be viewed in church.

The slides were pictures of other missionary families, half-dressed natives in gaudy clothes, pictures of tribal men wearing jewelry, pictures of bush houses, mud slides, flowers, and a picture where the natives worshipped. Mrs. Snustad was always nervous that she would see some heathen wearing her garden pedal pushers that she had put in the mission box.

After the missionary had put down his pointer and turned off the projector, he asked if anyone had any questions. Usually, only the kids had questions. They asked questions like: Does it snow? Have you ever ridden an elephant? Is it hot there? Do they mow the roofs of their houses?, and What do you do for Christmas? After questions were answered, the missionary told the people to come and look at the artifacts which he had displayed on a table. There were China Dolls, painted bowls for rice, African handicrafts from different tribes, kimonos, spears, Congo bongo drums and all sorts of things that weren't normally seen in Lutheran homes.

This is most certainly true.

The Mother-Daughter Banquet

Sometime between Easter and Pentecost, and between tulip and geranium seasons, the women of the Lutheran church sat down together in and amongst the mint green church basement poles around ten-foot, white-tablecloth-ed, lilac-bedecked banquet tables to enjoy their annual banquet. There was a committee to set the date and sell the tickets, a committee to plan the meal and the program, a committee to set up the tables and decorate, a committee to make the food and serve it, and a committee to take down the tables and clean up the kitchen.

The first two committees were the "Marys" of the church—the Ladies Aid president, the pastor's wife, and the "know it all" town women. They organized, but didn't do any of the real work. The last three committees were the "Marthas" of the church—the real troopers. They were the ones who kicked the legs out, pinched their fingers in the leg locks, and like strong men with sturdy backs, hoisted the heavy ten-foot banquet tables upright. They wiped down the chairs and set them around the tables using the lines on the linoleum as a guide to make sure they were straight. They unrolled the tablecloths and wiped them off, set the tables, prepared and served the food, cleared the tables, washed the dishes, cleaned up the kitchen, took down the tables, pinched their fingers again, stacked the tables up against the wall, wiped off the tablecloths, rolled them up, and took home the wet, limp, white dishtowels to wash.

Most women arrived promptly so they could find enough open places for their whole family to sit together.

Everyone was dressed in proper Lutheran attire. Some of the young mothers had sewn floral print or gingham-checked mother-daughter dresses for themselves and their young daughters. Some came in their Easter dresses, hats and gloves. Some young girls had on their spring recital dresses, and the teenagers sometimes wore the "home-ec review dresses" they had sewn.

One table might be full with five generations of Petersons from great, great grandma—who couldn't hear and basically had no clue where she was—to her two-week-old, fussy, great, great granddaughter who everyone could and did hear, but who also had no clue as to where she was. Another table might consist of Mavis, her five daughters, and four spinsters who had borrowed a daughter for the evening by paying for her ticket. Sometimes there were a couple of head tables reserved for the "Marys" of the church who sat proudly in their suits with their corsages, mothers' rings and attitudes showing. Of course if you had only sons, this banquet wasn't for you.

Mother-daughter look-a-like floral dresses

The program didn't vary much from one Lutheran church to the next. Devotions were given followed by a selection from the triple trio. Three of the pastor's wife's piano students performed at various times throughout the evening, one playing the *Minute Waltz* in two minutes and 45 seconds, one playing *Für Elise*, and the youngest playing *Bill Grogan's Goat* from John Thompson Book One.

There might be a flute selection from a graduating senior, but then again there might not. Several songs such as *Sweet Violets, Sweeter than the Roses, I Walk Through the Garden Alone*, or *Someone's in the Kitchen With Dinah* might be sung by all. If there was a really good Choral Reading Group in school, and they all happened to be Lutherans, they might be asked to do their reading—that is, if it placed with honorable mention or higher at the county level. The Ladies Aid president usually gave the mothers' tribute, and her teenaged daughter—who read too fast for the older ones—gave the tribute from the daughters. Sometimes cute poems were read, and sometimes serious things about motherhood and sacrifices were read. During the tributes or one of the musical selections, most were trying to look nonchalant as they munched on the mints and nuts that were placed —in pastel-colored May baskets or nutcups with pipe cleaner handles—to the right of their plates.

This banquet, prepared by the Marthas, usually consisted of curdled or uncurdled (depending on the cook) scalloped, Pontiac red potatoes and ham, peas or stringbeans (corn if the banquet was in Southern Minnesota, Iowa or Nebraska), cloverleaf rolls, a square of orange Jell-O that was filled with carrots and celery and topped with mayonnaise and a dash of paprika and parked on a limp lettuce leaf topped with a worthless sprig of parsley, pickles and a Dixie cup or a small scoop of orange sherbet garnished with two vanilla wafers that were standing straight as scarecrows in the garden. Coffee, milk and water were the standard beverages.

After the banquet, the Mary-type president thanked all the Marthas and everyone else, including the Marys who helped make the banquet a success. Before the closing prayer, the Lord's Prayer, and the singing of *Blest Be the Ties that Bind*, the last thing on the agenda was the awarding of the door prizes.

There were five basic categories awarded in any Lutheran church: the oldest, the youngest, who came the farthest, the one with the most generations present, and Mavis who always won for having the most daughters. Prizes usually were inexpensive, but useful such as a hanky, stationery, dusting powder or a little vase decaled with a Bible verse.

A good time was had by all.

This is most certainly true.

Excerpts from the Bulletin

It is time to clean the church for Easter and Summer weddings. If you belong to Naomi Circle, bring a mop and bucket and come Thursday morning at 7:00.

The Father-Son Banquet

Usually a month or so after Christmas, but before Spring planting was in full gear, the Men's Brotherhood had their annual Father—Son banquet. Unlike the women, the men didn't have to organize several committees to plan the banquet. They didn't cook the meal, plan the program, or clean up the kitchen. They just showed up with their sons who were old enough to eat on their own. As usual, the women did all the work.

There were no babies in attendance, no man who had only daughters, and no Norwegian bachelor farmers. (They just weren't good to clean up to go any place.) There were no door prizes awarded, no flowers on the tables, no nuts and mints nor any thought given as to what they should wear to this meal. They came to eat and since it was in the church basement, it seemed like basic Lutheran Christianity.

The menu was similar to the one served at the Mother-Daughter banquet, but the scalloped potatoes and ham portions were bigger, and they skipped the Jell-O. Instead, each was served two buns. And, instead of sherbet for dessert, they had cake and ice cream. The pastor usually gave the devotions, a ten-minute sermonette on what it meant to be a good father, and a couple of songs, such as *Viva La Compagnie* and *When Johnny Comes Marching Home*, were sung. Once in a blue moon, for variation, someone might play a cornet solo. They opened with the Table Prayer and closed with the Lord's Prayer. That was it.

No one thought anything about it until the next Sunday when the bulletin read: *Lost. One right rubber at the banquet. Contact Lars Pedersen if you have two right rubbers. He has two left ones.*

This is most certainly true.

Lutheran High Holy Days

There were three major high holy days in the Lutheran church for Norwegian, Finnish, Danish, and German Lutherans—and five for the Swedes. These were: Christmas, Easter, and Reformation Sunday celebrations for everyone—in addition to *Julotta* and *Sankta Lucia* Day for the Swedes.

The most memorable holiday for Lutherans was Christmas. There was the infamous Christmas program when good familiar hymns such as *Silent Night* and *Away in a Manger* were sung during services. The food in the basement was good and it was plentiful, and the tree in the sanctuary was lighted and it was beautiful, and it was *"mange takk"* to Martin Luther for starting this tradition.

Lutherans, including the Norwegian bachelor farmers, came to church at Christmas all dressed up in their best. It was velvet and taffeta, long white stockings hooked to garter belts instead of brown ones, and hats of fur and feathers. However, most importantly, A Child was born, and there was peace on earth and good will to all, including Widow Snustad—that is until the Annual Meeting.

The second major high holy day for Lutherans was Easter. It was festive in song and Word. Christ had Risen and so had some Lutherans who only showed up at Easter Services. There were trumpets blaring, and all the stops were pulled on the organ during the *Hallelujah Chorus.* The church was bedecked with white lilies and other spring flowers. The women wore fruit and flower-laden hats in colors of pink and purple, and dresses in pastel shades never seen at other times of the year in a Lutheran church. Little girls stole the Lutheran Easter parade show in their soft pink or blue shorty coats over see-thru nylon dresses. They fidgeted with their white lacy gloves and softly tapped their new patent leather shoes. They knew they looked cute. However, when they were adjusting their little white hats and the narrow little white rubberband chin strap snapped back and bit them in the neck, it smarted, and their minds were diverted away from themselves and back to the services. Little boys in suits, white shirts, ties and tan colored tweed top coats were just as cute, except they didn't like the attention, and they couldn't wait to get home and get those awful stuffy clothes off.

All shoes were polished for Easter, and so was the car.

Reformation Sunday, which was always celebrated the last Sunday in October, was the third most important high holy day on the Lutheran church calendar. It reminded us how lucky we were to be born into the right faith. Martin Luther's hymn, *A Mighty Fortress* , was sung with vigor, even though most Lutherans didn't have a clue what "a bulwark never failing" meant. Some Lutherans believed the celebration was meant to take our minds off Halloween. For Norwegians, costumes and Halloween–type antics were reserved for *julebukking*.

There was no special meal served on Reformation Sunday, but some, like Widow Snustad, felt that the color red should be worn by all good Lutherans on that most Lutheran of all high holy days.

Exclusively Swedish Lutheran

The *Sankta Lucia* Festival celebrated by Swedish Lutherans took place on December 13th. The Swedes borrowed this Italian saint, (who as legend goes, gave them food during a bitter famine), and used her as their mascot so they could legitimately eat *pepparkakor* earlier in December than the Norwegian–thus having one up on the Norwegians. Swedish Lutheran women were filled with horror and Lutheran guilt if they didn't have all their Christmas housecleaning done by December 13th, the day *Sankta Lucia*, the lady in white with the flaming candles on her head, would come like a *tomte* in the middle of the night and give the white glove test over all their furniture. Most Swedes tried to appease her by leaving a glass of *glögg* and a *lussekatter* out on the mantle for her. Others just left a note and asked her to dust.

Upon hearing about the religious overtones in the *Sankta Lucia* festival at Elim Lutheran Church, Widow Snustad said, "My, you'd think those Swedes would honor this lady who gave them food during the depressions by going without and giving it to the missions. But what do they do but feast on a *smörgåsbord*."

Another Swedish high holy day was *Julotta*. This Christmas Day morning service started so early that the farmers couldn't get all the chores done, and just had to let the cattle low. Swedish Lutheran women barely got the curlers out of their hair, and the children barely got the "the sleep out of their eyes" before the Mr. hitched up the horses to the sleigh, threw in the blankets, yelled "Giddy up, *Varsågod*," and got the family to church in time to sing *Var Hälsad Sköna Morgonstund,* see the lighted tree, and celebrate the birth of the Christ child. For Swedes it was as close to heaven as one could get on earth.

A Major Church Anniversary is a Minor Lutheran Church High Holy Day

When a Lutheran church was having a major anniversary, such as its silver or centennial, it was a milestone in the church that didn't go unnoticed. Committees were formed, programs were planned, historical notes, pictures and other interesting trivia from the records were printed and bound into a special yearbook and sold. Cookbooks, which included recipes from former pastor's wives and foreign recipes from missionaries, along with recipes for *lefse*, hotdish and cake recipes that were found in every other church cookbook, were written, put in a spiral bound cookbook and sold to help defray the cost of the anniversary celebration. Commemorative plates—which nobody liked and everybody bought for themselves and their children who had left the church—were ordered from some place in Iowa.

Former pastors, who hadn't been called home, were invited to come and preach, and to see how much the church had grown since they had left. The royal carpet was rolled out for former parish workers, Sunday School superintendents, and church organists. *Faith of our Fathers* was sung, and charter members and their offspring were given VIP treatment.

The church and its ground were spruced and cleaned up better than a Lutheran farm was before a firstborn's Confirmation. As Widow Snustad said, "I can't understand for the life of me why the church can't look this good all the time."

A Minor High Day That Wasn't So Holy

Every year, a Lutheran church budget was set in December, and a congregational battle was fought in January. It was the time of the year when the Pastor's proposed upcoming salary and what he did or didn't, or should or shouldn't, do was brought to light in the annual report.

It was the time of the year when everyone read the back pages of the annual report which exposed in printed word what everyone else in the church gave. It was the time of the year to discuss, debate and, for some Lutherans, to leave the church and start a new one. It was the only time Norwegian Lutherans showed Italian-type visible emotions. It was the pastor vs. the Widow Snustad-types vs. those who had strong opinions but weren't yet in the Widow Snustad camp. On and on it went until somebody from the kitchen hoisted the lunch counter window and yelled, "*Vær så god.*" After coffee and a couple of cookies, most Lutherans had forgotten what they were bickering about, put on their Kickerinos and overshoes and went home. But Widow Snustad didn't forget. She and the pastor both knew she would be in the parsonage bright and early the next morning.

This is most certainly true.

Men of the Church 1956

Who's Been Sitting in My Pew?

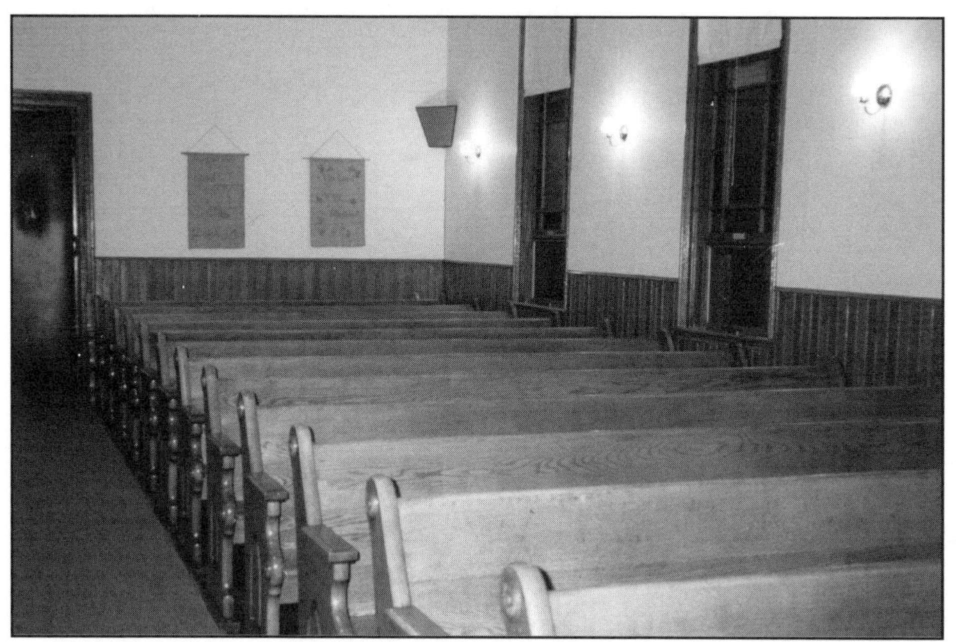

Ushers & Pews

Pew Protocol

The regulars knew the rules of the pew,
this is most certainly, certainly true!

Just like everyone in a family knew where to sit at the kitchen table when dinner was served, Lutherans knew where to sit in church. If you were a long-standing member of a Lutheran congregation, you had a regular pew. Nobody ever assigned it to you, but it was like squatter's rights; once you had been there so long, it was yours unless you came late at Christmas and Easter, and the two-time-a-year other members who didn't know the protocol sat down in your pew.

Some Scandinavian Lutherans believed that sitting in the same pew Sunday after Sunday was an inherent right. In some areas of Norway, "who sat where" was *rosemaled* on the sides of the pews. But, after the immigrants got over here, they were so busy clearing land and canning that no one had time to *rosemal*, so they just picked a pew and continued to sit there—sometimes from the fathers unto the children until the third or fourth generation . . .

Not only did Lutherans have their own pew, but they also knew who sat to the right of them, who sat to the left, who sat in the front of them and who sat behind them. They knew who sat in the middle of the pews and who sat on the ends, who would move over and who wouldn't. They knew who sat in the balcony, and who belonged in the balcony. Regulars knew that LUTHERANS DON'T SIT IN THE FRONT TWO PEWS. They knew who opened up the windows when it was stuffy, and they knew who had the guts to get up and close them a few minutes later. They knew who was having hotflashes and who was having a hard time. They knew who was the Avon lady and who had just finished with chores.

Regulars knew where the pastor's wife sat, where the Confirmands sat, and who besides Widow Snustad always complained about not hearing. They knew which mothers would let their kids bawl throughout the whole service disrupting everything, and which ones would get up and take their fussy babies out to the cry room where they belonged.

Regulars knew who snored, and who sat under the balcony—fourth pew from the back behind a pole to avoid the lights and catch a snooze. They knew who came early and who came late, and who the show-offs were who walked in right before the services started and paraded down the center aisle to the third row on the left side (as you are facing the altar).

Regulars knew who took off their coats and rubbers and hung them in the vestibule, and who sat all buttoned up like they were going out to shovel snow.

They knew who sang off-key, who sang too loud, whose voices were too squeaky, who just mouthed words and who harmonized during the singing of *Rock of Ages* and *Beneath the Cross of Jesus.* The knew which choir members had robes that fit, and which ones filled them out a little too much. They knew when the church organist was paying attention and when she was daydreaming.

They knew who gave generously, who gave with guilt, and who didn't give much at all. They knew who would usher, and which ushers would button the top button of their suit coat as they were walking up with the collection plate.

Regulars knew when the pastor had studied his sermon, when he should have spent more time studying his sermon, and just who in the congregation was the intended target of his sermon.

Regulars knew how many lights were hanging from the ceiling; the colors, shapes and pictures in all the stained glass windows, and who gave the money in loving memory of . . . for the hymnal that was in their pew rack.

Regulars knew when another regular missed, and the missed regular knew he would have to answer to the regulars the next Sunday when they would ask, "Was something wrong then?"

In other words:

Regulars knew the rules of the pew.

This is most certainly, certainly true.

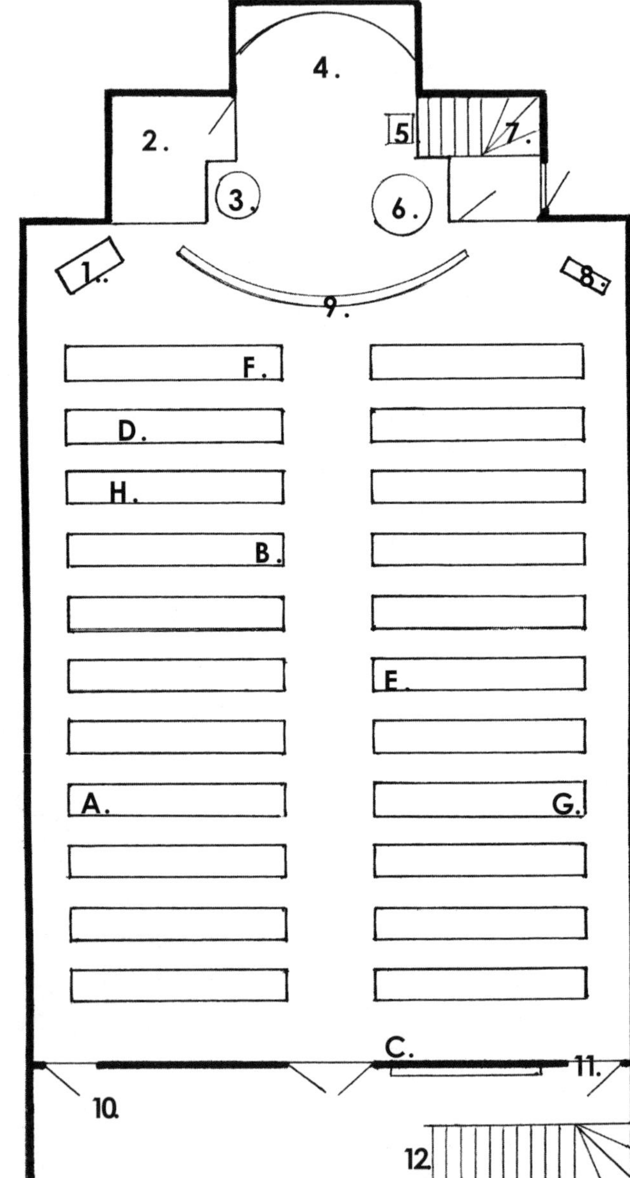

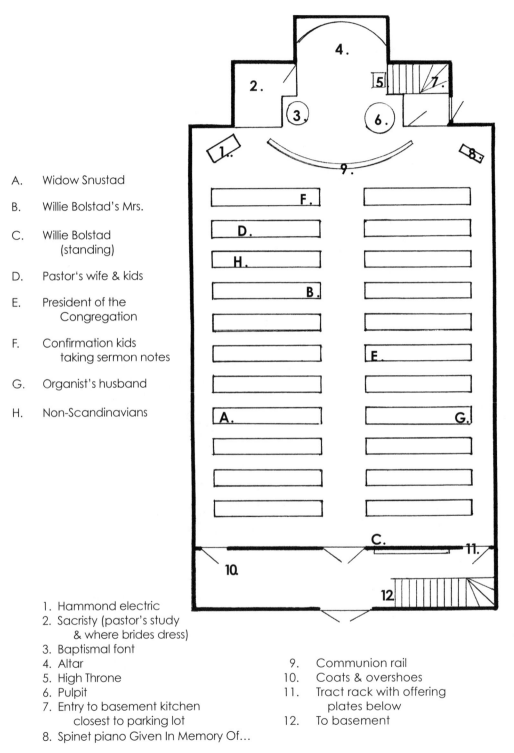

A. Widow Snustad

B. Willie Bolstad's Mrs.

C. Willie Bolstad
(standing)

D. Pastor's wife & kids

E. President of the
Congregation

F. Confirmation kids
taking sermon notes

G. Organist's husband

H. Non-Scandinavians

1. Hammond electric
2. Sacristy (pastor's study
& where brides dress)
3. Baptismal font
4. Altar
5. High Throne
6. Pulpit
7. Entry to basement kitchen
closest to parking lot
8. Spinet piano Given In Memory Of...
9. Communion rail
10. Coats & overshoes
11. Tract rack with offering
plates below
12. To basement

When the Plate is Passed and You Don't Put in Penger*

It was a given: "Even though we are justified by faith and saved by grace, there's Lutheran guilt we can't erase!" Dancing, playing with face cards, and enjoying Hollywood movies were not the only things chiseled into a Lutheran's own set of commandments. As Widow Snustad asked Pastor Lofsgaard early one January Monday morning after the church's annual report was out, "If they're not going to tithe, why do they even bother to come to church anyway?"

Getting Lutherans to be "cheerful givers" was not an easy task. When the immigrants came over from the Old Country, they came out of the state church which levied a tax to pay the church's salaries and upkeep.

The early Lutheran church tried the direct route too by telling individual parishioners what the church needed from them as far as money, chicken and eggs went. If the parishioner didn't produce, he was out of the church in two years. Some stayed, some were out. However, that approach didn't last.

The next approach they tried was public Lutheran guilt. It was called the Church Annual Report, and it came out every January. In the back of the report would be a list of what every member had given during the previous year. It was a way to shame those who hadn't given their fair share, and a way to thank those who had.

When the black hymnal was relegated to the church basement storeroom, so were annual reports with the "amounts given" lists. As Widow Snustad said sarcastically to Pastor Lofsgaard, "Well that's a fine Christian thing to do. Now they'll think they won't have to give anything!" But the Lutheran church decided it would try a different approach: generating private Lutheran guilt, and this is the way it worked.

As the organist played a foreboding hymn, the members

of the church would march single file around to the back of the altar and lay their solemn pledges in a collection plate. Like other approaches, this worked for some, but not for others. (Kids enjoyed going back there just to see what it looked like.)

However, the weekly collection plate had the desired effect. It nicely combined both public and private Lutheran guilt and kept it in the forefront. If you didn't put an envelope or money in the plate, the usher and everyone else in your pew knew. But if you did give, you would have to take up the matter of whether or not you put enough *penger* in the plate with God, and not Mrs. Snustad.

This is most certainly true.

**Penger is the Norwegian word for money.*

Excerpts from the Bulletin

A freewill offering will be taken next Sunday for the pastor. (It is a secret so do not let him know.)

The Ladies Aid will be meeting on Thursday, May 5 at 2:00 for its regular monthly meeting.

Rules and Duties of Lutheran Church Ushers

Requirements:

- For a *black* hymnal Lutheran Usher, a Lutheran usher must be:
  A member of the congregation he is serving
  A man
  Married
- For a *red* hymnal Lutheran Usher, a Lutheran usher must be:
  A member of the congregation he is serving
  A male
  Confirmed
- For a *green* hymnal Lutheran Usher, a Lutheran usher must be:
  Present or have lined up a replacement
  Other than that, anything goes.

Main Duties:

Functions can be roughly divided up into being a gatekeeper, the Welcome Wagon, and money changers. These functions can be broken down into four main categories of duties:

1) Welcoming (Handing out bulletins, seating strangers and lighting altar candles)
2) Offering (Collecting it and taking it to the altar)
3) Communion (Directing people, taking sign-up cards, refilling empties)
4) Dismissing (Letting people out, straightening hymnbooks, picking up)

Dismissing a congregation after a service is one of the most important tasks of an usher. This is where you earn your boutonniere. For heaven's sake, do not let the congregation tear outta there like a herd of cattle that have just eaten a patch of loco weed. Dismissal should be as orderly as the stacked silverware in the Ladies Aid kitchen drawers.

Two ushers are needed. Immediately after the Benediction has been pronounced, and just as the organ begins to swell, the two men should briskly march down the center aisle. Proceed to the front row. Turn to face the back of the church. (This is the only time it is acceptable to have your back toward the altar. Even during collection of the offering, try to face the altar head-on as you look and work to your side.)

Dismiss one row at a time. Each time the row of pews has emptied, step one step forward (towards the back of the church), almost in military fashion. If one side of the aisle empties before the other, wait for your partner's pew to empty. Step out together. Remain stately at all times. Nod to the person in the next pew to indicate that his pew may empty. For heaven's sake, do not talk to him. Continue in this manner until you and your usher partner have dismissed everyone. When everyone has been properly dismissed, proceed to your next duties: straightening hymnbooks and picking up bulletins, gum wrappers, and used Kleenixes from the pews and floor.

Miscellaneous Duties:

Depending on the church calendar, weather, attendance and other circumstances, a Lutheran usher should be trained to handle the following at the drop of a hat:

Finding hearing aids
Opening windows and closing them if the people seated by them don't
Stoking the furnace or adjusting the thermostat
Pointing out where the cry room or nursery are
Spreading out the hymnals during overflow
Nodding and pointing out the guestbook to stranger
Handling a coal furnace that starts to smoke
Putting up the proper hymn numbers on the wall if the minister or organist haven't

Chasing out birds and bats that may have entered when the windows were open
Bringing a thermos of warm water to church for baptisms

Possible Problems:
Be prepared to handle any of the following circumstances:
A crying baby whose parents won't bring him out
A runaway child
Coins that roll out onto the floor
A candle on the altar that goes out

Know ahead of time what to do if:
Someone takes a bit of time fumbling for his or her offering
Someone falls asleep and begins to snore. (Pay particular attention to the bachelors that are sitting in the back under the balcony)
Someone returns from Communion and goes to the wrong pew. (Communion can get a little punchy too. On a good day we can have up to five kneefalls at the altar. Don't let it turn into a circus.)
A kid gets dropped off for Sunday School and there isn't any

Collecting the offering:

There are several methods to employ in collecting the offering. These can be done with two, three or four ushers. Two is good, three is better and four is the best.

If there are only two ushers, they should stand in the center of the aisle (facing the altar) and hope that those seated on the wall end of the pew have enough sense to pass the plate back to the next row.

If there are three ushers, one stands in the middle aisle

and the other two are placed at the wall ends of the pews. The man in the middle does double time passing plates to succeeding rows. In this method you run the risk that a pew might get skipped from the center end.

If there are four ushers, the Lutheran ideal, two will be in the middle aisle and two at the wall ends. This method is a piece of cake. Only use two offering plates, though.

Hints:

Put your offering envelope into the offering plate before you begin collection so that the first people won't know if those before them gave or not. Do NOT put your envelope in when you are walking up the aisle either to collect the offering or to bring it to the altar.

Being an usher is an honor.* If the budget allows it, the congregation should purchase a white carnation boutonniere for the ushers to wear. This will help identify them to strangers. The boutonnieres should be kept from Sunday to Sunday on the shelf where the empty offering plates go.

Thank you for your service to the church,

Willie

Willie Bolstad,
Custodian and Head Usher

**Lutheran girls who were decent got to be Usherettes for John Deere Day in February. They got to carry a flashlight for the safety of those who came during the movie of new implements. Like being an usher in the Lutheran church, being an usherette for John Deere Day was also an honor. Only the nicest girls got picked by Floyd and Lloyd, owners of the local shop, and little Lutheran girls could hardly wait until senior high to see if they made the cut.*

Even When Steeples are Falling

Even When Steeples are Falling

Lutheran Church Architecture:
A Timeline in Color

Just as the Lutheran use of liturgical colors for the paraments, altar hangings, pulpit and lectern falls and the pastor's stole let people know what time of year it is, the changing architecture of Lutheran churches can also be coded by color.

Exteriors

White: This signifies the era of the rural standard church. Churches were white and they were wooden. There were two main steeple types, a squared-off flat-top one for the Swedish Lutheran churches and a long, pointed one for the Norwegian Lutheran churches. These buildings were wooden and painted white and the debates about predestination that occurred inside of them marked the beginning of merger-mania among Lutherans in America. German Lutheran churches were, of course, brick indicating the strength of their faith and the toughness of their demeanor.

Rust: Next came the era of English infiltration. Churches built during this era were brick and looked Methodist or Episcopalian. Controversy centered on the introduction of English or the retention of the mother tongue (Swedish, Norwegian or German—the language of the disciples) for liturgy. Splits and mergers continued to occur. Those who preferred English services split off and built new brick churches often in town, even though they were farmers. The mother tongue group retained the mother church. Lutherans who weren't involved in a controversy sometimes built brick churches during this era too because the original wooden one had burned down—a phenomenon rampant among Scandinavian Lutheran churches built by the settlers in the Midwest in the late 1800's, settlers who were at home with wood—and a cause of Lutheran ambivalency about Pentecost.

Pre-Red: Then came the wholesome era which is known for congregational togetherness, family life and red Jell-0. Outside the church, this fascination with red spread to barns in the country and lipstick in town. This circled around back to the church and was manifest by red nail-polished owner's initials painted on the cakepans brought to church and culminated with communism and the red hymnal.

The red hymnal era—the period from the 1960's to 1980— is also known as the era of more mergers and coincided with the beginning of the Lutheran era of interesting roof-lines and crosses in the 60's. During this architectural era, there were two camps: those who had some high church-low church-hymnal issues to deal with and those who spent time designing outlandish things.

Green: After the mid-70's not much time was spent building churches. Lutherans instead used the last half of the decade planning a new hymnal and selecting the color of the cover. The Green Era of Lutheranism began in 1980. Along with it came the era of contemporary music, guitars and passing the peace. Many conventional Lutherans, who were too tired to split and form another synod, simply joined another local congregation.

Interiors

Dark Brown: This era lasted until the late 50's At this time the last of coal burners had been replaced by a furnace. Indoor toilets were put in where the coal burner had stood. Of course, this meant that running water was also installed.

With soot being much less of a problem, Lutherans were free to lighten things up a bit so sanctuaries were painted beige and basements became mint green. As long as they were going to paint anyway, many congregations used the opportunity to rip out that dusty old pipe organ that was just taking up space and replace it with a modern, electric Hammond that even Luther League girls could play.

Blond: The 60's was marked and marred by social changes, hymnal changes and interior design changes. In this era of energy and "anything goes," many Lutheran churches underwent a complete makeover. Dark pews and altars were stripped, stained blond and padded. Center aisles upstairs, and linoleum floors in the church basement, were carpeted. The curtains that had been stretched on a wire between poles in the basement were taken down and portable, but tippy, Sunday School dividers were purchased.

Many Lutheran churches were remodeled to appeal to the masses now that a Catholic was president, and no one knew what might happen. Libraries replaced tract racks, overflow side rooms replaced balconies, fireside rooms were built and vestibules declined in importance. Cry rooms became nurseries complete with toys, an office (if there was one outside the parsonage) became the pastor's study, and the shuffleboard that had been carpeted over was replaced by a youth room that was never big enough. Sanctuaries were expanded so the electric Hammond could be replaced by a big pipe organ.

Although it wasn't intentional, building a fellowship hall was the most major design change of this era because it changed the whole social style and tradition of Lutheranism. With the new addition attached so close to the sanctuary, many congregations banned *lutefisk* and kraut dinners as they did not want the aromas to permeate the new carpet in the aisle. Overworked kitchen workers banned red Kool-aid (to say nothing about orange Watkins nectar) from the carpeted hall. With all the fancy kitchen equipment to operate it was often easier to call in some caterers.

Willie Bolstad was forced to put down his push-broom and take up vacuuming. Instead of ringing the bell on Sunday, he switched on the chimes. As he said to his wife after a long night of vacuuming up wedding rice, "Ja, I hope I live long enough to help them dig a basement under the church. You can paint the shuffleboard on, too."

This is most certainly true.

A Steeple Test

Before most of the Lutheran church splits and mergers over who knows what, it was quite possible to identify a Norwegian Lutheran Church, a Swedish Lutheran Church, a Catholic Church, and a Covenant Church. It was a little more difficult to distinguish among the Presbyterian, Methodist or Baptist ones, but it was possible. From 1965 and on, churches became kind of unisex—traditions blurred, and people had to start reading the signs outside the churches to know what kind they were.

In the 50's, some people out motoring tried to identify the years and makes of cars. Others tried to identify the religion associated with various churches. *This is a test.*

Circle the Norwegian Lutheran Churches, place a box around Swedish Lutheran and Covenant Churches, draw a line under the Catholic ones, place the first initial by the Presbyterian, Methodist and Baptist ones.

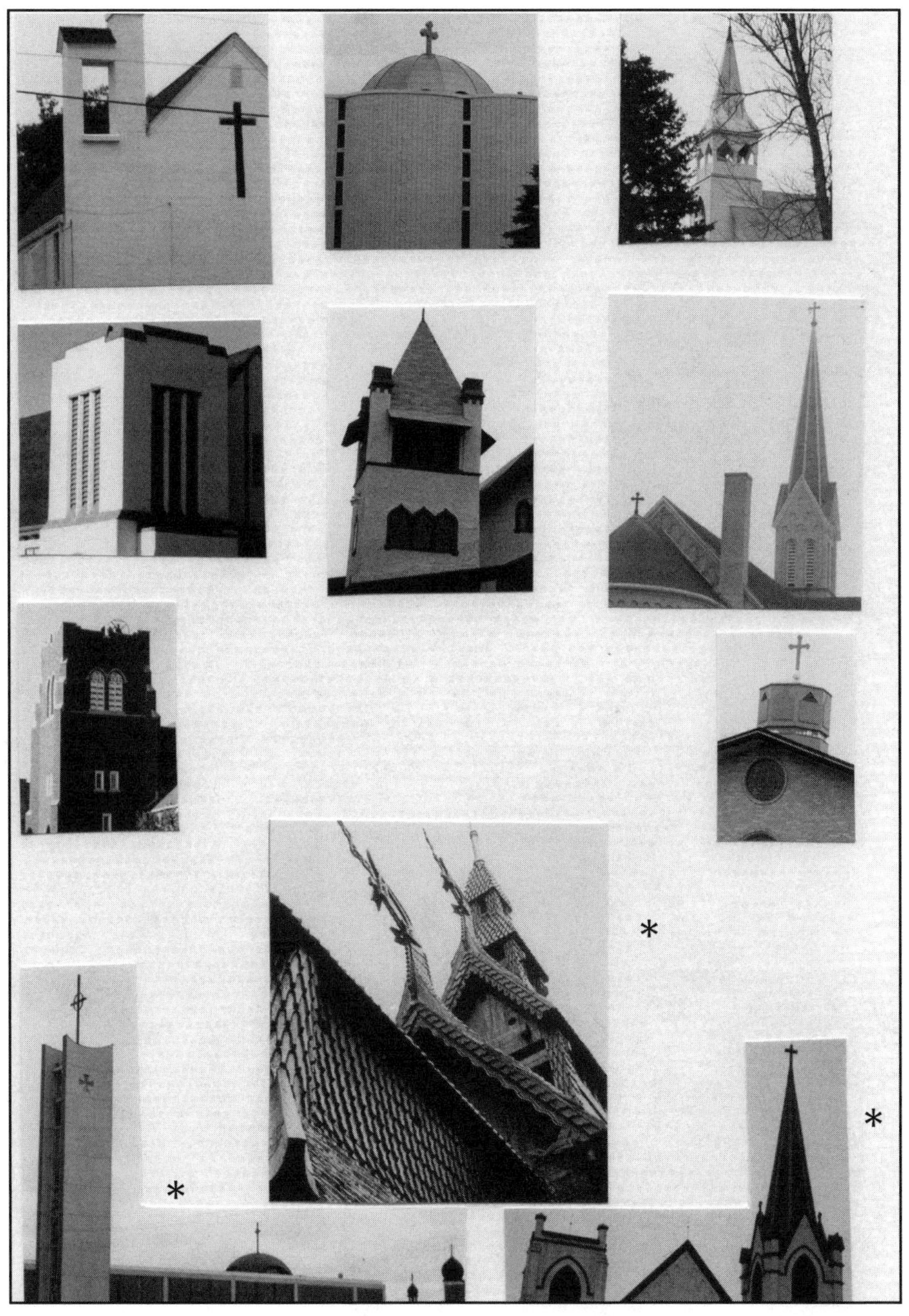

*These guys couldn't make up their minds

WYCLIFF
ST
FRANCIS
ASSISI

Harmony and Disharmony

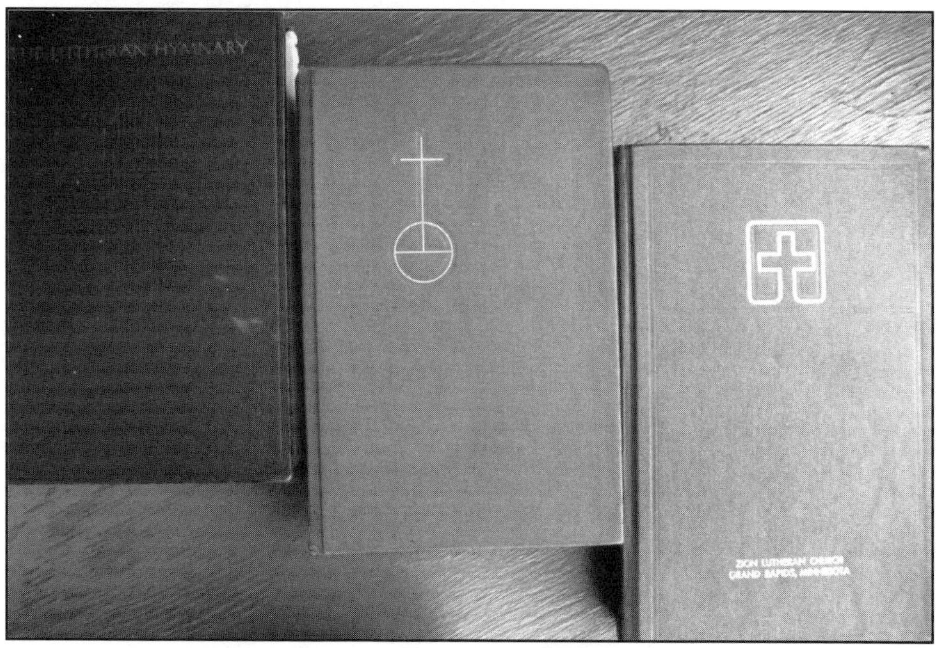

Music and Mergers

Lutherans Don't Come in One Size or Shape:

Physically, Lutherans come in all shapes, sizes and colors. They even sing about it: "Red and Yellow, Black and White, They are precious in His sight". There are Nice Norwegians, Stubborn Swedes, Robust Russians and Gigantic Germans. There are Chinese and Africans who were indoctrinated by Lutheran missionaries, and there are plain, old American Lutherans. Scattered in and amongst these flocks are a handful of Italians, Irish, Spanish, Mexican, etc.

Do different kinds of Lutherans believe the same things? Well, yes, basically the beliefs are the same, but the ways in which they are carried out — the What Does This Mean and How Is This Done stuff — vary considerably. All Lutherans sing *A Mighty Fortress* and no one kneels, but that's about all of the working procedures that Lutherans have traditionally had in common.

While all Lutheran kids memorized Luther's Small Catechism, Missouri Synod kids had to learn one more part than Scandinavian Lutherans did, the part about the Office of the Keys and Confession. Similarly, Scandinavian Lutherans were taught not to "deceitfully belie, betray, backbite, or slander" their neighbors and German kids were told not to "belie, betray, slander, nor defame" them. Missouri Synod kids couldn't join Scouts or go to Baccalaureate. Scandinavian Lutherans had better be at baccalaureate or risk congregational excommunication.

Martin Luther had taken care of the big debates, the things about Rome and indulgences, freeing up modern Lutherans to indulge in the details and daily workings of the church and its various congregations.

Like the number of synods, the proliferation of church buildings was about more than distance and convenience. So what if there were two Lutheran churches on one block, four churches at an intersection, or country churches of the same synod five miles apart. This was about last names and where grandparents were buried and, for Norwegian Lutherans, it was about the ease of forming a new church rather than discussing or disagreeing about an issue at the old church.

The art of splitting and merging really took hold with the Norwegian Lutherans in America. In the past 50 years or so, they have belonged to the ALC, ELC, LFC, LCA, AALC, EFCA, TALC, LCMS, AFLC, ULCA, ELS, ELCA, etc. Most likely Norwegian Lutherans will finally be in union with the other Lutherans when they finally form the AFL-CIO, the *American Federation of Lutherans Coerced Into One.*

For the last century, Lutherans in America have talked about unity and have claimed to embrace diversity, but often in rural reality the two concepts don't mix. Sometimes its just more comfortable to take things as they are and spend precious time drinking coffee, fanning oneself with a Sunday bulletin, and playing shuffleboard.

This is most certainly true.

For more information about what a "to do" all this merging stuff got to be, read "The Case of the Missing Merger Pamphlets" which tells how Aunt Wilma, who spent a great deal of time folding and stapling the pamphlet, "If God Had Wanted Us To Merge, He Wouldn't Have Created So Many Denominations To Begin With" in the Scandinavian- American mystery book by Janet Letnes Martin entitled Shirley Holmquist and Aunt Wilma: Who Dunit?

A German Lutheran choir in Iowa

Before & After Robes

Make a Joyful Noise But Do It In Four Parts, For Heavens Sake!

Lutherans are known the world over for their great choral tradition. Lutherans even have a national choir. College choirs from Augsburg College, Augustana, Concordia, Luther, St. Olaf, Gustavus, etc. practice and travel a lot serenading alumni throughout this country and kings and queens in foreign lands. This provides a good training ground for future church choir work.

Lutheran kids start singing as soon as they learn to talk. They have been singing voluntarily and involuntarily since they were three. By ages six and seven, Lutheran kids are reading music and singing harmony. (Those few who can't are giving antiphonal readings in up to four parts.) By the time the boys are eight or nine, they often have to be conscripted into choir by their parents and Sunday School teachers, but they do it and are better Lutherans for it.

By age ten, Lutheran kids are singing three-part music and by age twelve, they are singing four-part music, the foundation of the rich Lutheran choral tradition. For the next three years Lutheran boys try to disappear from the choral scene saying they have too much catechization stuff to memorize, but most Lutheran adults know better and don't push them. Therefore, Lutheran music for ages 12 to 15 is centered around the girls sextet, girls octet and the triple trio.

Organized choral opportunities prevail for little Lutherans. There are nursery choirs, preschool choirs, junior tots choirs, praise choirs, alleluia choirs and junior choirs. Choir practice and piano lessons will take up the bulk of Lutheran youth's free time. One of the real losses when a Lutheran "turns" is that he or she — given all their choral training and practice — is often reduced to singing one line of music or chanting.

As Lutherans grow older they have the Senior Choir

which enriches the Sunday service and gives Lutheran adults something to do on Wednesday night so they don't take up bowling. Some Lutheran singers run into a moral and theological dilemma when they get somewhere between 40 and 70 years old and making a joyful noise begins to differ from making beautiful music. The exact age varies as much as recipes for *rømmegrøt* do. Having grown up being taught that God gave them a talent and they should use it or it would be taken away, many adults are reluctant to give up choir even though it might be best for the other singers and the congregation. Of course, this isn't as much of a dilemma for the singer as it is for the director. Like Lutherans of every stripe, church choir directors like to avoid confrontation, and in an attempt to avoid pointing out the inevitable, the director often assigns minor solo parts to these people. That's why there are so many over-the-hill soloists in some Lutheran churches. Generally, Lutherans are very, very forgiving of anyone who can sing four-part music.

All of these beautiful four-part hymns are, of course, kept in a Lutheran hymnal, but where singing has created harmony among Lutherans, hymnals have created discord. Everything was as it should be in the Black Hymnal-Concordia era. These two hymnals provided a wealth of tradition (hymns by Luther, Grundtvig and Lindeman), and the services concluded with the threefold amen. Then, in the late 50's, something happened and Lutherans started changing hymnals as often as they changed the oil in their cars. Some said it had to do with Sputnik upsetting the sound waves.

At this time some bigshots at synod headquarters somewhere thought Lutherans should start learning some new hymns, but this was as futile as asking them to move out of their pew and sit in front. Lutherans started appointing people to various hymnal committees, a process that evoked as much discussion as the predestination controversy had with their grandparents. For many, it had the same results too. Individuals and friends broke off from the home congregation and formed new ones and new synods. The red hymnal was called too gaudy for a Lutheran church, and communist-inspired.

While many of the mainstay hymns made it into the red hymnal, others didn't. New composers' and arrangers' names showed up alongside of Gruber, Nicolai and Sandell-- names like Sateren and Christiansen. All of this was just an exercise, though, to prepare Lutherans for the changes that would eventually come with the green hymnal and With One Voice. With these latter two, memorized words to various hymns were changed. Everyone in attendance at Sunday services could guess people's ages by the words they sang to the familiar hymns. Again, new arranger's and composer's names crept in—names like Ylvisaker and MacKeever—and the organ would sometimes be drowned out by drums and guitars. As Willie Bolstad said to his wife after services on the day that the Gideon's had given their presentation, "Ja, we've sure strayed a long ways from Landstad's Psalmebog when fiddles were the tool of the devil."

This is most certainly true.

The Priesthood of Believers

DR. MARTIN LUTHER
Born Nov. 10, 1483
Died Feb. 18, 1546

Martin Luther: Hero? Heretic? Heritage!

Some kids who were of the eat-fish-on-Friday persuasion said that Martin Luther was a Catholic who, like a peach on a hot August day, went bad. Many other kids — those who are of the fair complexion, thick sweater, *lefse* or kraut persuasion — think that Martin Luther was kind of a disciple who was so busy pounding things that he forgot to attend the Last Supper. For several generations the debate has raged (rarely one-on-one; mainly on paper): Was Luther a hero or a heretic?

When Sandy Urness came home from Red Willow Bible Camp in 1956 she asked her father about this. Most Lutherans would have given the same response as Sandy's thick- sweatered, thick-skinned, thick-spectacled dad, Elmo, gave. "What kind of foolishness is that? Sounds like you had some of those guys just outta seminary teaching at Bible Camp. Now go pull some mustard and do something real for once." Real Lutherans, those who weren't going through puberty and questioning everything, knew the answer to this without wasting any time discussing it.

To herself Sandy wondered why it had been okay for Martin Luther "to turn" but not okay for Barbara Helgeson to turn when she married Buddy Verino from Chicago. Was Luther really from Germany and not Scandinavian? Why hadn't her parents, sponsors or Sunday School teachers taught her this? She felt betrayed, but like Mary, she kept all such things to herself and pondered them in the flax field while she was picking mustard.

These questions and a few others were answered a couple of years later when Sandy had lived through Public Questioning, finished Confirmation, received her Bulova, and was finally able to wear lipstick and nylons. Like most Lutherans who aren't planning to go to "the Sem," questions sort of stop after spending two years on Saturday mornings memorizing Luther's Small Catechism. After "reading for the minister" as her dad called it, life began to move so fast she hardly had time to think.

Of course, things went at a slower pace in the 1500's and Martin Luther had a lot of time to think and to question things. And, because he wasn't Norwegian, he even expressed his views right out loud to other people. Luther questioned authority; a very un-Lutheran thing to do. This, then, split the church in two. The Roman Catholics were on one side of the tracks (even though trains hadn't been invented yet), and the new Lutherans on the other. This practice continued for over 450 years when, if the tracks ran near the edge of town, the Catholics or Lutherans --whichever got there last--moved a few miles away and formed their own town.

Luther's invention of splitting has been a mainstay of Lutheranism, although in the past 150 years, Lutherans have added the concept of merging to this phenomenon. Splitting during the past three generations has not been caused by disagreement with the Pope. Recent splitting has been spurred on by more everyday matters. For example, Widow Snustad went into a snit when the Executive Committee of the Ladies Aid purchased new roasters without bringing it to a full vote. Willie Bolstad got a little huffy when the Property Committee, in cahoots with the minister, purchased padded seat covers for the pews. Willie wondered about the theological soundness of letting Lutherans get too comfortable in church.

Along with forming a new religion, questioning authority, pounding things and introducing the concept of splitting, Luther (called Martin Luther by Scandinavian Lutherans and Dr. Martin Luther by the German Lutherans) was also directly responsible for two other elements of Lutheranism: the power of the press, and the importance of good music.

The next coming split in the Lutheran church will likely revolve around the hymn and hymnal issue. Luther never wrote music for drums or guitars in church. Luther never wrote music for clapping. As Luther, himself, said: "Clapping belongs at ball games and political conventions, period." It is a well known fact that clapping breaks up the sacredness of a good traditional Lutheran church service. It wakes up sleeping babies and old men. Luther, the Preuses and the Youngdahls knew that taking up precious Sunday School space for cry rooms wouldn't be necessary if babies could sleep through the service. It was like Haybelly Hanson said, "If those newcomers who don't farm want to clap and sway and shout and make a ruckus, they can just go to one of those groups that meets in the gymnasium, or they can move down South." No one could argue with that and no one at Eksjø Lutheran wanted to.

Similarly, all of Luther's hymn compositions were written for four parts reflecting the Lutheran ideal of blending diverse sources into a harmonious whole. Of course, F. Melius Christiansen and his sons, apparently direct descendants of Luther, have carried this tradition on through this century. Luther and the Christiansens knew that if Lutherans spent their time singing there would be no time to use one's voice arguing. Besides, what was there to argue about? Luther had answered all the tough questions thereby freeing up succeeding Lutherans so all they had to do was keep to themselves, follow his teachings and enjoy the sensible Lutheran lifestyle.

Martin Luther knew that it was easier for a camel to pass through the eye of a needle than it was for Northern Europeans to express themselves. If he wanted his new religion to flourish, he had to find a nonverbal way of passing on Lutheran teachings and traditions, so one Wednesday night after Lenten services he invented the printing press.

Thus it was that Luther and his wife, Kitty My Rib (nee Katherina von Bora), packed up their brood and moved to Gutenberg. Martin spent many late nights assembling the press (batteries not included) and along about 9:30 every evening after the kids had said "Now I lay me down to sleep" and had been tucked in, Kitty would bring Martin a cup of Ovaltine and some bars. During his printing career, "bar time" was the only quality time Marty and Kitty had together.

As soon as the press was set up and the first Bibles were shipped out via Air Express to Scandinavian and UPS throughout Germany, Luther began his writing career and Kitty continued to bring him Ovaltine and bars. Kitty also had the task of dusting the press each Saturday morning just in case someone might drop in Sunday after services. Of course, if no one did, Kitty and Marty would load up the kids in the Packard and spend a few hours on Sunday afternoon driving around to look at the fields. Thus, another Lutheran tradition was established and it, like Kitty's bars, found their way to the Midwest centuries later.

Luther's habit of writing, printing and publishing was also transported to the Midwest. Initially, an extra press from Gutenberg that had seen its better days was shipped to Gettysburg, PA where the first Lutheran seminary had been founded. Soon presses in a variety of languages were set up for the hyphenated Americans. The German-American Lutherans established Concordia Publishing

House in St. Louis. The Danish-Americans rented a room behind the cafeteria at Dana College. The Swedish-American Lutherans had their print shop at Rock Island, Illinois and the Norwegian-American Lutherans set up Augsburg Publishing (named after one of Martin's hang-outs) in Minneapolis. The Norwegian-Americans thought it would be nice to have as many publications as there were Norwegian-American Lutheran Synods, and that there should be almost as many Norwegian-American Lutheran Synods as there were valleys in Norway. They continue to shoot for this goal today.

Starting small, the first published products were tracts and leaflets, and then catechisms and Bibles in a variety of European languages. Next these Lutheran businesses diversified into publishing bulletins, Sunday School books (often with silhouette designs), awards, and certificates for baptism, cradle roll, confirmation and marriages.

The most lucrative arm of the Lutheran printing businesses were the Lutheran magazine departments and the sheet music and hymnal divisions. Having committed the Sunday School song, "Red and yellow, black and white" to heart, the graphic designers and art majors employed by the great Lutheran presses tried to carry out this colorful theme on the covers of various hymnals. This practice continues to cause great concern among Lutherans today. Good Scandinavian Lutherans know that food is white, Communists are red, Christmas trees are green and Bibles and real hymnals are black. This is the way things always have been, are now, and ever shall be, so why try to be cute?

Lutheran magazines can be found in all Lutheran homes and, just like bread bags, they are never thrown away. Following Kitty's Lutheran Rite of Dusting the press every Saturday, Lutheran moms and kids (now that Confirmation classes are held Wednesday nights) dust the stacks of Lutheran Standard, The Lutheran, Lutheran Journal, Lutheran Digest, Lutheran Libraries, etc., every Saturday morning just in case someone might drop by Sunday after services.

Along with Luther's direct contributions—printing presses, beautiful hymns, the catechism and liturgy "in the language of the people"—were other indirect legacies that have defined the Lutheran heritage. Mainly, Martin Luther taught Lutheran kids like Sandy Urness what could happen if they didn't keep their ideas to themselves or if they tried to shake things up. From his experience, Lutheran kids learned to not say it even if they did mean it. Doing so could cast them in the limelight for centuries. Lutheran kids also learned the value of good choral music and good literature and not "to turn." Most of all, Lutheran kids learned not to question authority, just to take things as they are and not to get too excited. (The tradition of not questioning authority lasted at Lutheran colleges in America until the 1960's.)

To sum things up, Martin Luther defined the Lutheran tradition and heritage and it had nothing to do with being a hero or a heretic. It's just the way it was. He, like many others in different ways, were simply "called." The difference was that he listened and then acted. From Kitty, Lutheran women learned to dust and to make bars and to stay out of the way. Thus it was, is now, and ever shall be.

This is most certainly true.

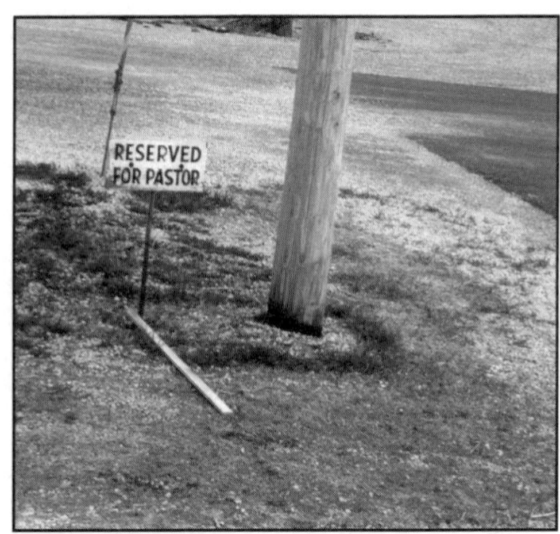

The Norwegian-by-Marriage Lutheran Sunday School Superintendent Who Had No Business Being One

Once upon a time there was a blond, long-legged, lanky Swedish-American girl named Linnea Annette from East of Grand Forks. Her folks have since moved into Forks and eat out all the time, and winter in Sun City playing shuffleboard and have even thought of taking up golf.

Linnea Annette grew up going to the Wesleyan Methodist Church in the country, and of course didn't have much in the way of Confirmation training because she didn't have to memorize Luther's Small Catechism by heart. As a matter of fact, being Methodist, she didn't have to memorize much of anything. She just sort of showed up at services, dressed in blue and yellow, and acted like going to church was nothing too special.

Linnea married Harv Olufson after the cultivating was done in the year of the big flood in the big valley in the '51. Good thing for Harv, too, that there had been cultivating to do because his dad, Alvin, was plenty upset with Harv for marrying outside the faith. Alvin, who had been a Lutheran, in good standing, all his 63 years, resigned himself to the fact by imagining that it could have been worse. Linnea could have been Episcopalian, or Harv could have been in the service and come home with one of those Italian war brides who liked things tomatoey, wore shoes with straps all over them, and was Catholic through and through.

It was sticky and stuffy and muggy in that little country Methodist Church that stifling hot June day as Mrs. Hazel Mattson, in her high-pitched annoying voice, sang *O Perfect Love* and *Entreat Me Not To Leave Thee.* Linnea had, naturally, chosen her high school classmates to be waitresses for the church basement reception. They were all nervous that their white, starched organdy aprons

Linnea had made them by hand were going to wilt and get all wrinkled. Linnea's Aunt Esther, the one who was on the heavy side and had recently had a blood clot in her leg, and was pouring coffee and afraid she'd stick to the chair. Beulah, the bride's mother, was afraid that her new Dacron dress would be soaking wet right through when she was ushered up the aisle. Joyce, the mother of the groom, could not have cared any less about the whole thing and just wanted to get it over with, go home and take off her Sunday girdle, and put her feet up.

The hot sticky wedding day was, in a way, an omen of the bride's life to come. Never one to get hot and bothered about church loyalty, Linnea continued to attend Wesleyan Methodist. Sometimes Harv went with her, but usually he went with his folks to Mt. Carmel Lutheran. When Linnea's parents moved to Grand Forks, Linnea decided she might as well join Harv and his family to save some gas.

Well, the women of Mt. Carmel, feeling haggard and overcome with the myriad of responsibilities that accompany being a lifelong Lutheran woman, were always on the lookout for new blood and unanimously voted in Linnea Annette as Sunday School superintendent. Linnea Annette, who took church life as casually as she took aspirin for a headache, thought this would be a good way to win over her in-laws and agreed to assume the responsibility.

It was smooth sailing for about two days, but then the wind came out of Mt. Carmel's sails. The ladies of the church felt like Peter, James and John in the boat. A storm came up, a tempest brewed, the seas rolled, and the boat capsized. The tempest came in the form of Widow Snustad who marched over to the parsonage and demanded to see Pastor Brandvold and to see him *now*! "Just what is this world coming to?" she demanded. "Is nothing sacred anymore? That woman, selected to be spiritual head of our Sunday School program, hasn't ever memorized Luther. She wouldn't recognize a Catechism if it landed in her lap. In all my 74 years of faithful membership in Mt. Carmel, this takes the cake. Now what are you going to do about it."

Not wanting to create waves and rock the boat, and not wanting to listen to Widow Snustad anymore, Pastor Brandvold asked her if she felt the Lord was calling her to take the position of Sunday School superintendent. Widow Snustad had really gone overboard this time and she knew it. Shaken, but still trying to be polite, she thanked Pastor Brandvold for his confidence in her and reminded him of how much her rheumatism had been acting up. Widow Snustad thanked him for his time and his excellent suggestion. Then she hustled home, grabbed the hotwater bottle and, for the first time in many years, kept to herself for three days.

Linnea Annette, who never caught wind of this whole ordeal, is in her 36th year as Sunday School superintendent at Mt. Carmel this year.

This is most certainly true.

The Lutheran Church Hierarchy

Martin Luther
The Preuses, Youngdahls, Strommens, Forbes, Christiansens, Noreliuses, Muuses, etc.
Bernt C. Opsal, Reuben Gornitzka, Pastor W. E. Klawitter on the radio
Billy Graham (Honorary Lutheran)
Synod Headquarters Folks
Congregational Pastor
Pastor's Wife, Janitor, Ladies Aid President, Sunday School Superintendent, Organist
Trustees and Deacons, Deaconesses, Choir Director
John Ylvisaker and Nelson Trout
Garrison Keillor (Honorary Lutheran)
Released Time Teachers, Finance Committee
Sunday School Teachers, Cemetery Board
The Priesthood of Believers

A Catechism for Conventional and Contemporary Lutherans

This is an explanation for newcomers to the Lutheran church. It will help them learn the difference between the Jell-O and Hotdish Lutherans and the hand-clapping, liturgical dance ones.

A Conventional Lutheran...

- continues to search for the word "coffee" in the Bible.
- considers wafers more holy and Christian than bread hunks.
- feels that the phrase "Lutheran Bishop" is an oxymoron.
- knows that real Confirmations are held in the Spring and not in the Fall.
- thinks the Apocrypha is a monument in Greece.
- visualizes manna as miniature *lefse.*
- thinks "Moderation in all things" is a Bible verse.
- knows what "to turn" means.
- figures that the only proper place for a common cup is out in the field passing the water jug.
- thought immigrant grandparents spoke in tongues.
- would rather vacation in South Dakota than Italy.
- regards *Children of the Heavenly Father* as the most beautiful song in the world.
- wears a suit to services in the summer even if there is going to be a visiting minister.
- wishes the trustees would do something about the pastor's daughter being a cheerleader.
- secretly wonders just who goes downtown to the local hard liquor store to buy the communion wine.
- is pretty sure that all the pairs of animals in Noah's Ark were married.
- would rather have the older, narrower bulletins

without all the inserts for less conspicuous hotflash fanning during the "11 o'clock."

- kind of thinks that Billy Graham, the Lennon Sisters and Princess Kay of the Milky Way are Lutherans.
- gets a little uncomfortable when women bring the collection up to the altar.
- has an aunt who has been in a Triple Trio.
- prefers the King James Version and silent prayer.
- thinks the parsonage is a public building.
- really did "Read it Through in '62".
- has a last name that ends in *...son, sen, nes, berg, holm or land.*
- knows which hymn is on page 141 in the yellow, spiral-bound Youth's Favorite Songs.
- likes the old bulletins with a colored picture on the cover better than the black and white sketchy ones nowadays that come in the wrong size anyway.
- can name at least three Lutheran Synods and which people left in a huff, but can't tell you the theological differences among them.
- thinks the Annual *Lutefisk* Supper is a Lutheran Feast Day and considers John Deere Day a church event.
- feels farmers are closer to God than city folks.
- knows that Heaven is up and Hell is down.
- refers to the devil as "Satan" when in public.
- feels pastors got more respect when they wore black robes.
- would be a somewhat more comfortable if people who drive pickups to church would park a little farther away.
- remembers when she saw her first nun.
- can pronounce names that begin with *Bj* and *Kn.*

- sings the right version of *Away in a Manger.*
- feels that Passing the Peace is a little too touchy.
- thinks acolytes aren't necessary because we're paying the pastor to do that stuff anyway.
- knows how to make egg coffee.
- feels that clapping and laughing out loud are more appropriate in auditoriums than in the House of God.
- thinks tuna hotdish is okay but fish sticks are too ecumenical.
- still calls it the *new* red hymnal.
- assumes that *lutefisk* and *lefse* are directly descended from the two fishes and five loaves at the Sea of Galilee.
- craves beverages that come from a Watkins bottle.
- wonders whether or not the pastor takes note if you choose the wine rather than the grape juice.
- believes all angels have blond hair and cheese cloth gowns.
- figures any pastor's wife worth her salt knows how to play the piano and the Flut-o-fone.
- finds flannelgraphs, chalktalks and filmstrips more acceptable than liturgical dance, drama and drums in church.
- knows that real hymns have four parts and any thing printed with just the melody line is only a song.
- finds Rook, shuffleboard and musical chairs (to the tune of *All Hail the Power*) acceptable forms of entertainment for Christians.
- belongs to a church that keeps the funeral table cloths in a special drawer.
- gives old bathrobes to the Sunday School superintendent to be used by the shepherds.

- wonders why Luther Leaguers always have to travel so far away to become better Christians.
- remembers exactly when he got his first Bulova, what it was for and who it was from.
- wonders if things weren't better when you gave the minister two dressed-out, dead chickens and a ham rather than a pension.
- gets nervous when the phrases "voluntary prayer", "testimony" or "altar call" are mentioned.
- never had a male Sunday School Teacher.
- sometimes slips and says Holy Ghost instead of Holy Spirit, trespasses instead of debts, Creator rather than Maker, and the holy Christian church rather than the holy catholic church.
- calls the minister Pastor Olson, not Pastor John.
- knows what it feels like when the Jell-O melts into scalloped potatoes on a paper plate.
- has a tough time with the idea that ministers procreate.
- has a soft place in his heart for the navy blue "Concordia".
- understands why *The Beautiful Isle of Somewhere* was banned even though the melody wasn't too bad.
- can't figure out why the other synods just don't get it.
- gets a little nervous watching filmstrips of the mission fields for fear that the pedal pushers she gave to the clothing drive might show up on the screen.
- prefers not to read Song of Solomon 4:5 or Exodus 20:17 out loud.
- prefers not to have Song of Solomon 4:5 or Exodus 20:17 read out loud.
- got gold stars for "learning things by heart."

- knows that the Top Three funeral hymns are *Den Store Hvite Flok, How Great Thou Art,* and *The Old Rugged Cross.*
- female has a designated pair of funeral shoes for serving.
- thinks the laying on of hands belongs in Crusades, not in services.
- thinks swaying and waving one's arms in church is the work of the devil.
- has a drawer full of organdy aprons, just in case.
- sometimes uses Lutheran, Christian and Protestant interchangeably.
- recognizes that there must be a place for New Wave Lutherans but wish it wasn't in their own congregation.
- skips the Homecoming Dance even if she is the queen.
- thinks Garrison Keillor is a Lutheran wanna-be.
- thinks the most Lutheran animals are sheep, dove and fish, and that the most Lutheran musical instruments are pianos, organs and flut-o-fones.
- remembers when the old-fashioned pipe organs were replaced by modern, electric Hammonds.
- believes that if Jesus were living on earth today, he probably wouldn't drive a turbo or clap his hands in church.
- has carved crosses out of Ivory Soap bars from craft class at Bible Camp or VBS.
- is pretty sure God is a male, and Jesus is of European ancestry.
- says "Oh, he looks so natural" at funerals and then keeps to himself.
- considers mint green and beige as proper church basement colors and considers "hymnal red" too gaudy for church.

- thinks Pinã Colada is one of Columbus's ships.
- never gave Episcopalians much thought before August 1997.
- surmises that the Concordat is either a kind of grape or a graduate of a liberal arts college in Minnesota or Nebraska.
- thinks those hotshots at synod headquarters can get a little high falutin' sometimes.
- knows what the following letters stand for:
  VBS PTR YPS INRI SS KJV LCR
  ALC WMS WCTU ELC LCA RSV
  TALC LL LDR AAL LBI ELCW
  CLBS LB and WELCA.

A Contemporary Lutheran...

- knows what WOV* stands for and strives to put this concept into practice.

This is most certainly true.

* *With One Voice; another new Lutheran hymnal.*

Acknowledgments

Technical Advice: Carol Frick
Silhouette Illustrations: Oletta Wald

Special Photography: Kathleen Bade

Bethel Lutheran Church
Madison, WI

Photo Credits:

Laying the Cornerstone, p. 195
North Dakota Institute for Regional Studies
North Dakota State University

Holden Lutheran Church (125th Anniversary Book)
Kenyon, MN

Faith Lutheran Church
(A Century of Faith Centennial Book)
Forest Lake, MN

First Lutheran Church (Centennial Book)
St. Paul, MN

East and West Zion (Centennial Book)
Starbuck area, MN

Miami National Luther League Convention Book-1961

A special thank you to the congregations and individuals who let us take pictures of them, to the individuals and congregations that submitted photos, and to the friends and relatives who didn't know that we were going to use pictures of them.

ABOUT THE AUTHORS

Janet Letnes Martin – native of Hillsboro, ND and now a resident of Hastings, MN – and Suzann Nelson who – grew up near Evansville, MN and now lives in Grand Rapids, MN – met at Augsburg College in Minneapolis during Freshman Week of 1964. To this day they remain two "100 percent Norwegian-American Lutheran Farm Girls Who Didn't Turn!"

Martin has co-authored several bestselling humor books with Allen Todnem; *Cream and Bread, Second Helpings of Cream and Bread,* and *Lutheran Church Basement Women.* In 1996, she compiled a heritage cookbook with her sister, Ilene Lorenz, called *Our Beloved Sweden: Food, Faith, Flowers and Festivals.* Martin has written *Shirley Holmquist and Aunt Wilma: Who Dunit?*, and *Helga Hanson's Hotflash Handbook,* and has designed several humorous products: *Helga Hanson's Hotflash Hanky, Helga Hanson's Hefty Hauler, Red Jell-O Queens* dishtowels, egg coffee mugs, and *Lutheran Jell-O Power* aprons.

Nelson officially teamed up with Martin in 1994 to write *Cream Peas on Toast: Comfort Food for Norwegian Lutheran Farm Kids and Others;* a Catholic — Lutheran Lexicon called *They Glorified Mary, We Glorified Rice;* and a Farm kids — Town kids Lexicon entitled *They Had Stores, We Had Chores.* Nelson also edits books, including *Our Beloved Sweden.*

In 1996, Martin and Nelson wrote and published *Uffda, But Those Clip-ons Hurt ,Then!* and a compendium of rural Midwestern farm phrases entitled, *Is It Too Windy Back There, Then?*

Along with this book, *Growing Up Lutheran: What Does This Mean?,* Martin and Nelson are compiling a companion volume called *Picture This,* a "photo album" of Lutheran life in the 1950's.

Martin and Nelson, individually and together, are very much in demand as humorists. They speak about their experiences growing up in rural Norwegian-American Lutheran communities.

ORDER FORM

GROWING UP LUTHERAN

Name____

Address_____________________________________

City______________ **State**__________ **Zip**________

No. of copies ____@ $13.95 Subtotal $ ________

Plus postage & handling:
1st Class: $3.95/book or 3rd Class: $2.50/book
Maximum postage $10.00 $______

MN Residents add 6.5% Sales tax $______

TOTAL $______

Send check or money order to:
CARAGANA PRESS
P.O. Box 396
Hastings, MN 55033
Or Call (800) 797-4319 or (800) 494-9124

OTHER BOOKS published by Caragana Press:

- You Know You're a Lutheran If...
- Just How Much Scrap Lumber Does a Man Need to Save?
- Luther's Small Dictionary: From AAL to Zululand
- Uffda, But Those Clip-ons Hurt, Then!
- Is It Too Windy Back There, Then?
- They Had Stores/We Had Chores
- They Glorified Mary/We Glorified Rice
- Cream Peas on Toast